Serpent
of
Wisdom

About the Author

Donald Tyson (Nova Scotia, Canada) is an occult scholar and the author of the popular, critically acclaimed *Necronomicon* series. He has written more than a dozen books on Western esoteric traditions.

Visit him online at DonaldTyson.com.

Serpent
of
Wisdom

AND OTHER ESSAYS ON WESTERN OCCULTISM

Donald Tyson

Llewellyn Publications
Woodbury, Minnesota

FIRST EDITION
First Printing, 2013

Cover art: Abstract aged paper: iStockphoto.com/Kim Sohee
             Snake and magical symbols: Dover Publications
Cover design by Ellen Lawson

Llewellyn Publications is a registered trademark of Llewellyn Worldwide Ltd.

Library of Congress Cataloging-in-Publication Data
Tyson, Donald, 1954–
   Serpent of wisdom : and other essays on western occultism / Donald Tyson. —
First Edition.
      pages   cm
   Includes bibliographical references and index.
   ISBN 978-0-7387-3618-1
1. Occultism. I. Title.
   BF1411.T97 2013
   130—dc23
                                    2013002526

Llewellyn Publications
A Division of Llewellyn Worldwide Ltd.
2143 Wooddale Drive
Woodbury, MN 55125-2989
www.llewellyn.com

Printed in the United States of America

Contents

Introduction

A TIME OF CHANGE

We are living in a time of great change. Some might argue that every period in history is a period of change, that change is the only constant, but there is something different about our time. The change is not so much taking place in the external world in the form of technological advancement. That outward form of change has been going on since the dawn of the Industrial Revolution, and we have become accustomed to it. The present change is internal, and it is taking place within us. Western civilization is questioning the very roots of its existence. The beliefs and convictions that held true for many centuries are currently under assault, not just by intellectuals in the rarefied realm of academia, but by ordinary men and women, who find that they can no longer accept many of the certainties of former generations.

This transformation in attitude shows itself in the rejection of many of our long-established institutions and customs, but

1

nowhere more clearly than in the rejection of mainstream religion. Christians are turning away from the churches in large numbers. Atheism is at an all-time high. The Vatican cannot find enough priests to say mass, and monasteries and nunneries are closing down simply because there are not enough of the faithful to sustain them. People no longer turn automatically to the churches for marriages, christenings, confirmations, and burials. Sunday has become just another day of the week.

The controversial magician Aleister Crowley believed that his text *Liber AL vel Legis* (*The Book of the Law*), which he received in a psychic dictation from his guardian angel Aiwass in 1904, marked the beginning of the transition between the old astrological Age of Pisces and the new astrological Age of Aquarius. Each of these astrological ages, which are measured by the sun's slow movement backwards through a zodiac sign, lasts approximately 2,200 years. The transition from one age to another is not a sharp transition, but a slow evolution that may last for a century or longer. It is said by astrologers that such transitions are always distinguished by chaos, as the old ways give way to the new ways. So, even though Crowley thought that the very beginnings of this transition were in 1904, the change from the Age of Pisces to the Age of Aquarius is still taking place.

Crowley associated the old Age of Pisces with Christianity. It was his revelation in *The Book of the Law* that the transition to the new age would be marked by violent transformation and disruption, as the old ways and old beliefs were cast aside before the new ways and new beliefs had yet been fully formed. Crowley called the new Age of Aquarius the Aeon of Horus, after the Egyptian hawk-headed god of war. The old Age of Pisces he called the Aeon of Osiris, after the Egyptian god of death and rebirth. In his view, both world wars were merely manifestations of the chaotic change predicted in his prophetic *Book of the Law*.

We don't need to be followers of Crowley's personal cult of Thelema to see that something dramatic is happening to Western civilization. The 20th century was one of the most warlike in history and saw the introduction of atomic weapons, a method of killing on a mass scale that had never before existed in the entire history of the world. Yet most of the changes during the past century were outward changes. We had the advent of the automobile, the airplane, and space travel, to say nothing of television, the computer, and the Internet.

Since the millennium, that change has become more internalized, as we ourselves change to reject the past, without yet having a clear view of our future. It may have been the Internet, introduced in the final decades of the 20th century, that accelerated this crisis of belief. With instant access to all human knowledge, and instant communication with everyone else in the world, many minds that had previously been asleep began to wake up. They saw the faults and limitations of the old beliefs about spirituality, morality, and social interaction, but they have not yet settled upon a new set of beliefs. The result is a very restless and uncomfortable generation that seeks conviction and spiritual comfort wherever it can find it.

One of the curiosities of our dawning new age is the popularity of the ancient esoteric practices of the West that we call occultism or magic, particularly among young people. Magic is the most conservative of all disciplines. Its modes of practice have not changed in any appreciable way in thousands of years. Yet in this chaotic time of transition between the old age and the new, the occult has offered us an alternative to the dying churches by giving us a structure of spiritual beliefs that is not in immediate and fatal conflict with our modern view of reality.

It really is surprising that magic, the most ancient and primal of all human studies, should be perceived by the young as more modern and more suited to our new century than established religion, yet the great popularity of occult studies testifies to it. The spiritual truths of Hermetic philosophy, alchemy, the Kabbalah, and other esoteric streams nourish the human spirit in ways that the churches, synagogues, and mosques have lately failed to do. The reaction in the West against a rising tide of materialism is not, as might be expected, a return to traditional religion, but rather an experimentation with esoteric philosophies of the same sort that were taught by the Egyptian priests and Greek Neoplatonists.

Why is magic more suited to our new age than religion? In part it must be because magic offers many varied paths to spiritual enlightenment, none of which is considered absolute or superior to all others. There is no list of "thou shalt nots" in Western magic. Some occult disciplines are as chaste and ascetic in their practices as any Christian monastery, whereas others revel in sexual excess—and both paths lead to truth. It is up to the seeker to choose which path is best for him or for her.

It is a curious truth that cannot be denied that Christianity came into being roughly at the beginning of the astrological Age of Pisces, more than two thousand years ago, and that the Roman Catholic symbol of Christ is a fish, just as the meaning of the zodiac sign Pisces is the Two Fishes. It is another curious truth that Christianity seems to be failing just as the Age of Pisces is coming to a close, and giving way to the Age of Aquarius, the symbol of which is the Water-Bearer. Aquarius is understood in astrology to be the zodiac sign of intellectual clarity and freedom.

It has been my life's work to examine different aspects of the Western esoteric tradition, and to reinterpret them in order to make them both clearer and more accessible to modern readers. I have been doing this for almost forty years, all the while practicing these same techniques in my own life. Many people who turn to the practice of magic in order to realize important goals, or just to achieve a deeper understanding of their own nature, find the sheer mass of the ancient teachings a bit daunting. They don't know where to begin. This collection of essays is designed to provide an overview of some of the more vital topics of Western magic, and to present them in a way that will make sense to educated 21st-century readers. Let me help you to understand the basic principles of Western magic.

Most of the essays in this collection were written between 2006 and 2009 for the online magazine *Rending the Veil*. They are not too technical for the average reader—indeed, they were written with the beginner in mind. At the same time, they offer a unique perspective on these important esoteric topics that will be new even to those with a more extensive understanding of the occult. Those familiar with my books know that I am never content with just regurgitating existing information—I want my readers to actually understand what I write on a deep personal level, so that it makes sense not just in a dry intellectual way, but as something they holistically embrace and make their own.

A FEW DEFINITIONS

Before I introduce the individual essays, I need to give a few brief definitions to place them in their proper context. Unfortunately, common dictionaries are not up to the task of defining the terms used by modern magicians. Dictionary definitions of esoteric terms tend to be vague and circular—by circular I mean that term A is used to define term B, and then elsewhere term B is used to define term A. For example, in *Webster's New World Dictionary*, witchcraft is defined as (among other things) sorcery; yet if you look at the definition for sorcery, you will find it defined as witchcraft. These circular associations have some value but are not enough in themselves for a complete understanding of occult terms.

What is Western occultism? It is an ancient tradition that combines practical magic used for causing changes in the greater world with contemplative disciplines that are intended to perfect the mind and spirit. The occult tradition of the Western world has its roots in Egypt, Judea, and Mesopotamia. It was evolved and unified in ancient Greece, and further refined by the Roman Empire, which carried it throughout Europe in the train of its advancing legions. The European empires that arose from the Renaissance spread the Western occult tradition around the world, to the Americas, Australia, New Zealand, South Africa, and countless other locations where Europeans settled. The magic we use today has not changed greatly in the last five centuries.

Occult simply means what is veiled or hidden. Western magical practices are called occult because at one time they were done in secret to prevent persecution from the courts of justice and the Christian churches. Today, the practice of magic is in the open, and anyone can learn it who seeks it out. Magic is no longer a forbidden activity, and is no longer against the law in most places in the world.

Another, more subtle reason to refer to magic as an occult practice is its tendency to conceal itself in plain sight from those who scorn it. Even though magic is now available to everyone who seeks it out, only a few whose minds are open to its mysteries will reap its full benefits. Magic is a precious gem that lies in a busy street, covered in mud. Most people will walk past it without giving it more than a momentary glance, or will kick it aside with the toe of their boot, but those who bend to examine it more closely will find its beauties revealed.

The occult tradition is often called by the alternative title, the esoteric tradition. *Esoteric* is what is confined to an inner circle of initiates. This used to be the case with magic, but today anyone who seeks to learn its methods can find thousands of books on the subject, some quite good and others not so good. But there is another sense by which magic may be called an esoteric discipline—not because it is withheld from seekers by a circle of initiates, but because so few who seek to learn it are ready both intellectually and emotionally to receive its wisdom. There is an old saying, "You can lead a horse to water, but you cannot make it drink." In our modern Internet age, the water of esoteric wisdom is everywhere, but few drink deep of its springs.

Our Western tradition, which descends from Judea, Mesopotamia, Egypt, Greece, and Rome, and involves the practice of such things as alchemy, astrology, numerology, Kabbalah, and ritual spirit evocation, is in contrast to the Eastern esoteric tradition of India, China, and other Asian nations, which is based in part on such disciplines as Indian yoga and Tantra, the Chinese Tao and tai chi, Japanese Zen, and Tibetan Buddhism. Eastern occultism relies extensively on exercises in breathing, posture, meditation, and chanting.

There is a general philosophical difference between the occultism of the West and the East. Western esotericism tends to focus more on the outer world, and Eastern esotericism more on the inner world. The magician of the West relies more heavily on external tools and materials to achieve his purposes, whereas the magician of the East uses his own mind and body. This is not an absolute distinction, but only a general difference in attitude between West and East. Neither esoteric tradition is better than the other. At root, all magic around the world is one. It comes from the same source, and works in the same way.

With the enormous rise in popularity of hatha yoga and tai chi in Europe and North America, and the increasing numbers of Westerners who engage in Eastern meditation, the average person may not realize that the West has its own rich esoteric tradition that is every bit as ancient and as powerful as that of the East. One of the purposes of these essays is to introduce various powerful and transformative aspects of Western magic to those who may be completely unfamiliar with them.

THE ESSAYS IN THIS BOOK

The first essay, "Definition of Magic," shows just how inadequate dictionary definitions really are in expressing the meaning of so complex a word as *magic*. The attempts to define magic are traced down through the centuries from Pliny the Elder, who lived in the time of the Roman Caesars, to Aleister Crowley and those who followed after him in the 20th century. By bringing together into one place all the ways in which scholars and practitioners have tried to pin down the meaning of magic with words, a greater understanding is achieved of the evolution of magic as a concept. Yet in the end, the essence of magic, its defining core, can never be fixed into place. How do you define the indefinable? Like an elusive butterfly, magic forever remains alive and free.

After examining what magic is and what it is not, we take a look at the single most important tool used in ritual magic. "The Magic Circle" is an in-depth analysis of the meaning and use of the circle in Western magic. At first consideration the circle may seem too simple a thing to require an essay, yet though it is central to Western magic, it has seldom been rightly understood, even by those who use it daily in their ritual work.

At the very heart of traditional Western magic is communication with and command over spirits. If you look at the old grimoires of magic, they all have one thing in common—they describe methods of making contact with spirits and commanding them. Yet what is a spirit? There are many opinions. "The Nature of Spirits" presents some of them, and attempts to get at the root of what spirits are, why they bother to interact with human beings, and what they really want.

Western occultism is filled with powerful symbolism, and with mythic themes that run like golden threads through the fabric of the centuries. The essay "Serpent of Wisdom" looks at the role of the serpent in the magic of the West. The serpent in various forms, such as that of the wise and deathless snake, the dreaded basilisk that freezes its prey motionless with a glance, the flying serpent, and the fire-breathing dragon, appears prominently in the magic of both East and West. Why are serpents so universally linked with the secret wisdom traditions?

Common to both witchcraft and ceremonial magic is the familiar spirit that serves, teaches, and protects its master. The essay "Familiars" examines the origins and uses of familiar spirits. There is the common misconception that the familiar of a witch is a pet animal. This is not so—the familiar of a witch is a spirit that dwells inside a pet beast, ready to emerge when commanded by the witch. Magicians often placed serving familiars in inanimate objects such as rings or crystals. Here we examine exactly what a familiar spirit is and why it was regarded as so essential in traditional Western magic.

There has been an enormous explosion of popular interest in vampires over the past few decades. Beginning with Bram Stoker's *Dracula*, and continuing more recently with Stephen King's book *Salem's Lot* and Anne Rice's vampire novels, the fascination for vampires shows no sign of ending with the enormously popular *Twilight* series of novels by Stephenie Meyer. "Vampires, Werewolves, Ghosts, and Demons" looks at the true nature of vampires, and the almost-equally popular werewolves, from an occult perspective, along with the true nature of two other popular subjects of novels and movies: ghosts and demons. These creatures do exist, but they are not quite as they are represented in popular novels and movies.

"Guerilla Divination" shows that almost any set of simple objects can be used to divine the future and things hidden, provided we know the basic principles of divination. For this essay, I created a completely new system of divination that uses the common coins that everyone carries in their pocket, and I explain the principles that underlie all forms of divination by the fall of lots. This is more than just a simple and practical method of divination that you can use in your own occult work—this essay explains the basic structure of all divination by the fall of lots, allowing you, if you wish, to design your own methods of divination.

The essay "Sensory Metaphors" is probably the most important essay in the book, because it deals with the perplexing question of what is real and what is unreal. Many people dismiss the occult out of hand merely because they fail to understand that the reality of spirit beings is not a gross physical reality. Here we look at the way in which a nonphysical entity can appear completely physical to all the physical senses, and why there is such confusion about the reality or unreality of ghosts and other spiritual creatures. The term *sensory metaphor* is one that I coined in order to explain how something can seem physically present in every way, yet not be physically present, and why all efforts to photograph or otherwise record spirits with machines are doomed to failure.

The "Order of the Tarot Trumps" is the most advanced essay in this book, in a technical sense. The earliest decks of Tarot cards were unnumbered. When they began to acquire numbering centuries ago, different sequences were adopted for different Tarot decks. Occultists have been debating with one another since the close of the 18th century what the true order of the picture cards of the Tarot should be. The order we usually accept today is based on tradition. Various great men of magic, such as Éliphas Lévi and Aleister Crowley, advocated changes in the sequence of the twenty-two picture cards known as the trumps. Here, I look at their ideas and how they caused the sequence of trumps to evolve in the Western tradition, and then I present my own sequence of the Tarot trumps and explain why it seems to make the best esoteric sense.

In the brief essay "Time and Magic" we take a look at the true nature of time and consider its implications for the modern practitioner of magic. A magical perception of time liberates the consciousness and also helps to explain various puzzling occult phenomena such as precognition and déjà vu.

The essay "The Fairy Godmother" was written to show that there is much of practical value that can be learned from myths and legends, if they are examined in the right way. The stories about fairy godmothers are especially fascinating. Fairies are not tiny creatures with insect wings, as Disney movies might cause you to assume, but powerful spirits of the earth and of the dead who have interacted with human beings for thousands of years. They have been especially prominent in the lore of the Celtic peoples, but they are not creatures of the dim past. They exist today, and can be contacted through magic.

The essay "Black Magic" deals with the somewhat contentious questions of what black magic is and whether it even exists. Some modern practitioners assert that there is no black or white magic, only shades of gray magic. Devout Christians, on the other hand, like to assert that all magic is black, whatever its nature. Here I take the view that magic is neither black nor white in itself, but only becomes differentiated into these traditional categories by its intended purposes.

"The Book of Spirits" examines an extremely important tool of traditional Western spirit evocation that was extensively used during the Renaissance in Europe. It is a book the pages of which are designed to actually capture and embody spiritual creatures, so that by opening the book to the page of a particular spirit, and conducting a ritual of evocation, that spirit is made to appear visibly. The book of spirits is still used today by a small number of more knowledgeable magicians, but few who claim to have skill in the practice of magic understand its making and use, or its potency.

In "Esoteric Energy" I deal with the very important question of what composes the actual force that manifests itself during works of ritual magic. It is not a physical energy—if it were, it could be measured by machines, and this is not the case. However, it causes physical changes in the world by a reactive process. This magical force has been recognized to exist throughout human history. The Chinese called it *chi*, and the Polynesians called it *mana*. In spite of its many names, it is always the same. It expresses itself as a blind force of nature, similar to electricity in the sense that it has no morality, but can be used for purposes good or evil.

The essay "Spirits' Rights: A Manifesto" is a brief work in which I set forth my reasons for believing that spiritual beings have dignity and rights that should be respected by human beings, even as we respect the rights of other people. My years of dealing with spirits have shown me that they have feelings that can be injured and pride that can be bruised. It is morally wrong to treat spirits as no more than servants or slaves. In our Western culture some groups have advocated extending rights to animals, in the recognition that they can think and feel. The next logical step is to grant rights to spirits as well.

The final essay in the book has the distinction of being the single most controversial piece I have ever written. It is titled "The Enochian Apocalypse Working" and was published in *Gnosis Magazine* (Summer 1996). Since then it has been reprinted several times in anthologies. It sets forth the speculation that the Enochian angels who visited the Elizabethan sage Dr. John Dee had an ulterior motive for transmitting to him the system of Enochian magic—that it was intended by the angels to trigger the apocalypse described in the biblical book Revelation. Dee himself never understood this purpose, which lay dormant for many years, but I speculate in the essay that Aleister Crowley, who considered himself the Great Beast of Revelation, may have worked Enochian magic in such a way as to begin the process for which it was originally intended. I do not believe Crowley completed what I call the Enochian Apocalypse Working, but I suspect that he may have begun it, and may have opened the doors of the Watchtowers just enough to provide a hint of what is to come.

Conclusion

In these brief essays, I have tried to open windows of understanding on various important topics of Western occultism, presenting them from the perspective of a practitioner who grasps the subject not only in an academic way, but firsthand as an actual user of magic in his daily life. All too often occult topics are disparaged in mainstream magazines and newspapers, on radio and television, and from the pulpits of the churches, by those who know nothing about them. This causes the general public to get a completely false understanding of what magic is and how it may be used.

Western magic is not only a spiritual discipline of the highest order, capable of enlightening the mind about the true nature of self and its place in the universe, but a practical tool that can be used in daily life by anybody to realize desired life goals. During this time of great change, when the foundations of beliefs that supported our culture for centuries are crumbling away beneath our very feet, magic offers an alternative to an arid and cynical materialism that denies any higher or unseen power. Those who work magic know that such a higher force exists, because they can feel it working and see its results in their daily lives, as they bring about improvements in themselves and their environment.

As the old Age of Pisces gives way to the new Age of Aquarius, and the old truisms and convictions and certainties crumble into a chaos of confusion, it may be that the oldest of all spiritual disciplines, the practice of magic, which is older and more primal than the practice of religious worship, will provide a bridge on which to stand that religion has failed to give us. Magic existed before Islam, before Christianity, before

Judaism, before any religion, and it still exists today, untarnished by the centuries, as potent as it ever was.

Those who work magic are doing the same things that shamans did ten thousand years ago, and they get the same results. Magic gives us today what it gave those honored dead—control over our lives, a sense of our true place in the universe, and a vantage on the realm of the spirits, which is not some strange and distant place, but exists all around us, interacting with us and interpenetrating our reality from moment to moment.

The way of the West is the way of the warrior. The magician faces the dawning new age without doubt, secure in the knowledge that what was so at the beginning of time is still true. Societies may change, civilizations may rise and fall, religions may come and go, but magic is eternal. It is a wellspring of wisdom and power that never fails, a constant from age to age. As it was in the beginning, so it is today, and so it will be at the end of things. Those who embrace its truths have no fear of change.

1

Definition of Magic

MAGIC HAS TWO FACES

Magic is one of the slipperiest concepts in the English language. No definition seems to satisfy all requirements, and there have been numerous definitions over the centuries. In my opinion, the word has never been adequately defined, and perhaps never can be, but it is informative to examine the attempts that have been made by the writers of dictionaries and by various scholars and magicians.

We are concerned here with occult magic as opposed to stage magic. In ancient times all magic was occult or supernatural. Stage illusions went by other names, such as *legerdemain* and *jugglery*. Contrary to popular belief, the figure in the Tarot trumps known as the Magician is actually the Juggler or Mountebank—a stage performer of deceptive tricks that give the illusion of magic. The early French term is *Bateleur*. Another French name for this trump was *Le Joueur de Gobelets* (The Cups Player). The stage magic trick of the cups and balls goes back to ancient Egypt. The Italians called the figure on this trump *Bagatino*, a word meaning "a trifle" that is also the name of a comic character of Italian popular theater.

There was confusion as to whether the performances of the traveling jugglers of Renaissance Europe were real, illusory, or a combination of both, and this doubt spilled over to the Tarot trump of the same name, so that it came to be associated with real magic, stage magic, and a combination of the two. The ambivalence concerning the magic performed by the figure on this Tarot trump reflects in microcosm the larger confusion about magic in general—is it real, is it fraud, or is it a mixture of both?

Dictionary definitions of magic fall into two categories: those pertaining to real or occult magic, and those that describe stage magic, or trickery. The confusion of these two types of magic has in part been responsible for the ill opinion that grew up around it. Magic and trickery became synonymous in the minds of the average person, and the mighty mage of old was often reduced to the status of a carnival performer.

How the attempt to define magic is approached depends, more than any other factor, on whether the person defining magic believes it to exist. The writers of dictionaries do not credit the existence of magic. Hence they rely on a lot of qualifiers such as "seeming" or "supposed" or "pretended," as in this definition from *Webster's New World Dictionary*:

> 1. the pretended art of producing effects or controlling events by charms, spells, and rituals supposed

to govern certain natural or supernatural forces; sorcery; witchcraft.

2. any mysterious, seemingly inexplicable, or extraordinary power or influence: as, the *magic* of love.

3. the art of producing baffling effects or illusions by sleight of hand, concealed apparatus, etc.

In its earliest beginnings, there was no confusion about this term. Magic was simply the art of the Magi, the priest cast of Persia renowned throughout the ancient world for both their wisdom and their occult abilities. The wise men who are described in the New Testament as traveling from the East to visit the crib of the baby Jesus were historically assumed to have been Persian Magi, who had by their arts foreseen the birth of the Christ (see Matthew 2:1). Christian tradition from the sixth century gives their names as Casper, Melchior, and Balthasar, but nothing certain is known about them.

PLINY THE ELDER

Yet even this identification of magic as the art of the Magi is less simple than it appears, for some of the ancients held magic in highest reverence, while other disdained it. Pliny the Elder (23–79 AD), who actually lived during the time of Christ, in Book XXX of his *Natural History* wrote that the Greek astronomer Eudoxus of Cnidus (409–356 BC) "wished magic to be acknowledged as the noblest and most useful of the schools of philosophy."[1] The inventor of magic was said by Eudoxus to have been the Persian mage Zoroaster, who was believed to have lived 6,000 years before the death of Plato (who had been a teacher of Eudoxus). Pliny wrote that Aristotle confirmed this assertion by Eudoxus.

By contrast, Pliny himself held magic in contempt and applauded the efforts of the Emperor Nero (37–68 AD) to expose it. Nero had Persian Magi at Rome teach him the secret arts of magic, but he finally gave them up in a fit of frustration, declaring them all to be no more than liars. It is doubtful that it ever occurred to Nero that he himself might be unworthy of the arts, though the thought undoubtedly passed through the minds of his Persian teachers.

Pliny divided the Persian magic into three branches, those dealing with medicine, religion, and astrology. He also recognized another type of magic practiced by the Jews, but declared it to be thousands of years more recent in its origins than that of Zoroaster. He also mentioned "Cypriot magic" as more recent—this may have been a kind of witchcraft.

The first book on magic, so far as Pliny could ascertain, was one written by the sage Osthanes, who had traveled with Alexander the Great (356–323 BC) to the East on his campaign of conquest. Pliny wrote: "One thing is certain; it was this Osthanes who chiefly roused among the Greek peoples not so much an eager appetite for his science as a sheer mania."[2]

Pliny mocked the legends that the great Greek philosophers had all traveled to Persia to study the arts of the Magi. It is quite possible that many Greek sages made this journey, since the Magi were renowned for their knowledge of astrology, which of all occult arts was held in the highest esteem in the ancient world. Such travels were not uncommon, as the biography of the Greek magician Apollonius of

Tyana makes plain. Apollonius was said by his biographer Philostratus to have traveled to Egypt, Persia, and even to India in his search for occult knowledge.

With the rise of Christianity, definitions of magic became more censorious. Whereas Pliny mocked magic mainly because he believe it to be a fraud, the early Christian writers reviled it as an art of Satan himself that could only be used for works of evil. They did not doubt the reality of magic, but tended to regard it as wholly devilish.

THE BOOK OF ENOCH

The *Book of Enoch*, a pseudepigraphical text that was originally written in Aramaic around two centuries before the birth of Jesus, concerns a group of angels known as the Watchers. These angels were sent by God to observe the Earth and the doings of humanity, but they began to lust after mortal women and descended to this world to couple with them (I Enoch, ch. 6):

> And it came to pass when the children of men had multiplied that in those days were born unto them beautiful and comely daughters. And the angels, the children of the heaven, saw and lusted after them, and said to one another: "Come, let us choose us wives from among the children of men and beget us children."[3]

This is mentioned briefly in Genesis 6:2, where the Watchers are called "sons of God." They were actually Archons, gods equal in nature to God himself, who was not different from them in kind, but was their leader, the Chief Archon. This is how they were able to rebel against God in civil warfare. They would not have been able to do so had they been only lower creations of God.

The Watchers taught their children by these women many forbidden arts, including the arts of magic. We would be more inclined to call these arts sciences and crafts. Some are listed (I Enoch, ch. 8):

> Semjaza taught enchantments, and root cuttings, Armaros the resolving of enchantments, Baraqijal taught astrology, Kokabel the constellations, Ezeqeel the knowledge of the clouds, Araqiel the signs of the earth, Shamsiel the signs of the sun, and Sariel the course of the moon.[4]

With this knowledge at their command, the descendants of these Watchers, the "mighty men which were of old" mentioned in the Book of Genesis, conquered other lands and ruled the world. "And as men perished, they cried, and their cry went up to heaven."[5] (I Enoch, ch. 8.) In punishment, God sent the flood to destroy most of the human race, and he exiled the Watchers themselves to an abyss beneath the earth.

This is the same event as the rebellion of the angels in heaven and the fall of Lucifer, although this is not widely recognized. The rebellion in heaven and the descent of the Watchers to breed on mortal women are two aspects of the fall of the angels. Lucifer's rebellion was his attempt to teach mankind the arts and sciences of heaven. The same myth is echoed in the Greek myth of the Titan Prometheus, who was punished by Zeus, leader of the gods, for attempting to give mankind the gift of fire.

This myth, meaningful in so many ways, illustrates the attitude toward magic that was held by the Christian Church of the Dark Ages and Middle Ages, an attitude which naturally conditioned the definitions of magic given by the early Christian writers. Saint Augustine's definition in Book XXI, chapter 6, of the *City of God* is typical: "magic art, that is demonic arts performed through human agency, along with miracles wrought by the demons themselves."[6] He went on in the same chapter to write:

> And that men may provide these attractions, the devils first of all cunningly seduce them, either by imbuing their hearts with a secret poison, or by revealing themselves under a friendly guise, and thus make a few of them their disciples, who become the instructors of the multitude. For unless they first instructed men, it were impossible to know what each of them desires, what they shrink from, by what name they should be invoked or constrained to be present. Hence the origin of magic and magicians.[7]

In the opinion of Augustine, the root of magic was instruction directly from devils to men. This is in accord with the myth of the Watchers, who taught their children and mortal wives forbidden arts, that is presented in the *Book of Enoch*. It colors, or perhaps I should say that it stains, all definitions of magic that came out of the Christian theologians and demonologists.

THE *DAEMONOLOGIE* OF JAMES

When King James the Sixth of Scotland (1566–1625), who would later be crowned James the First of England, came to write his treatise on witchcraft, titled *Daemonologie*, he did not doubt the existence of magic, but he regarded it as a deception and a snare of the Devil to catch fools and the wicked. He was a learned man, and he naturally went back to the classics of Greece and Rome for his background on magic, but he interpreted the opinions of the ancients through the filter of Christian religious mania (*Daemonologie*, bk. 1, ch. 3):

> This worde Magie in the Persian toung, importes as much as to be ane contemplator or Interpretour of Divine and heavenlie sciences: which being first used amongs the Chaldees, through their ignorance of the true divinite, was esteemed and reputed amongst them, as a principall vertue: And therefore, was named unjustlie with an honorable stile, which name the Greekes imitated, generall importing all thes kindes of unlawfull artes.[8]

James divided magic into two general types, both unlawful in his view: necromancy and sorcery. In modern times this general division is commonly called high magic and low magic. He associated necromancy with the learned classes, and sorcery with the ignorant classes. Witches were grouped with sorcerers. The primary distinction he made was that the necromancers command the devils to do their bidding, but that the sorcerers are commanded by the devils:

Surelie, the difference vulgare put betwixt them, is
verrie merrie, and in a maner true, for they say, that
the Witches ar servantes onelie, and slaves to the
Devil; but the Necromanciers are his maisters and
commanders.[9]

Despite this distinction, which James in general acknowledged, he regarded both groups as ultimately slaves to Satan,
since the necromancer has power over devils only by virtue
of his black pact with them. The primary example of this
view is the story of Faust, a German scholar who made a pact
with the Devil and was given a personal demon as a servant
who carried out all of Faust's wishes. At the end of his life
Faust was dragged down to hell to be forever damned.

How great is the gulf between this narrow and bigoted
view of magic and that held by the earlier Neoplatonists of
the Greeks, who wrote about the Egyptian art of god-mak-
ing, by which the Egyptian priests induced the intelligent
essences of deities to descend to earth and inhabit and ani-
mate physical images, which became oracular. The Egyptians were said to have actually commanded the gods, and
even to have created them in a sense, by manifesting them
in physical objects. Yet James dismissed the same art of
magic as nothing more than devil worship.

James was remarkable for his intolerance and narrow-
mindedness. He was happy to let the great English philosopher and magician John Dee starve and would cheerfully
have had him executed had it been convenient for him to
do so, but he was frustrated by English common law, which
gave the learned Dee some protection, even in his extreme
old age and mental infirmity. James hated Dee because Dee

represented the highest and most noble form of magician, the occult philosopher, defined by Cornelius Agrippa in his *Three Books of Occult Philosophy* and exemplified in Agrippa's own life. Dee was the living proof that not all magicians were evil—yet James did his best to cast Dee in that light, and repulsed all petitions for aid by the aged magician, even though Dee had been the trusted personal advisor to the former monarch, Queen Elizabeth. Had James known the full extent of Dee's commerce with the Enochian angels, the king would certainly have had Dee arrested and executed, but those dealings did not come to light until after Dee's death.

RALEGH'S *HISTORY OF THE WORLD*

Not all the learned men of the Renaissance were as benighted with religious fanaticism as James. Sir Walter Ralegh, or Raleigh (1552–1618), in his 1614 *History of the World* wrote more sympathetically about magic, even though he quoted the recent treatise on witchcraft by James with great respect (not that it saved him—James eventually had him executed). Ralegh repeated from Pliny and the other ancient authorities the belief that magic was the invention of Zoroaster and had descended from the Magi of Persia, but was skeptical on the matter (*History of the World*, bk. I, ch. 11, sec. 1):

> I do not think that Zoroaster invented the doctrine of the horoscopes or nativities; or first found out the nature of herbs, stones and minerals, or their sympathetical or antipathetical workings; of which I know not what king of Chaldea is also made the inventor. I rather think that these knowledges were far more ancient, and left by Noah to his sons.[10]

Ralegh alludes, of course, to the myth of the fallen Watchers in the *Book of Enoch*—that the knowledge of magic was first given to humanity by angels, who were punished for this transgression by God, just as humanity was punished by the Flood for having received the gift.

Ralegh divided magic into lawful arts and unlawful arts. This was the general view of his time among the learned of Europe, though it was not held by the religious fanatics, who tended to view anything connected with magic as devilish. He stated very explicitly that the magic condemned by King James was indeed of the Devil. He gave four general classes of magic, based on a biblical text: "Daniel, in his second chapter, nameth four kinds of these wise men; Arioli, Magi, Malifici, and Chaldaei." He then went on to describe these four types (bk. I, ch. 11, sec. 2).

He wrote that of the first type, the Arioli, the old Latin authors translated *sophistas*. These were the philosophers, naturalists, and wise men of the ancient world. He quoted Vatablus: "For the magi are the same with the barbarians, as the philosophers are with the Grecians, that is, men that profess the knowledge of things both divine and human."[11]

The second class from the biblical book of Daniel, the Magi, "our English call astrologers" but Saint Jerome and the Septuagint Bible called them "magicians."

The third class, the Malifici, are wholly evil in Ralegh's view. He called them "*malifici*, or *venefici*;" in the Septuagint, witches or poisoners. They are those who, "without any art of magic or necromancy, use the help of the Devil to do mischief."[12]

The fourth class, the Chaldaei, are those who "took upon them to foretell all things to come, as well natural as human, and their events; and this they vaunted to perform by the influences of the stars, by them observed and understood."[13]

It will be apparent that this classification is rather muddled. Astrology is referred to in both class two and class four. The Magi and Chaldaei would seem to be much the same thing. Perhaps they can be distinguished by saying that the Magi were the actual priest caste of Persia, whereas the Chaldeans (as ancient writers, and Ralegh used the term) were merely Persian astrologers, and a larger group that contained the Magi as a subgroup. Although, it might be counterargued, the secrets of the Magi were unlikely to be given to those outside the priest caste.

There is also a confusion over natural and supernatural practices. Poisoning in itself is not magical. In the Renaissance it was closely linked to witchcraft. Witches were believed to be agents of the Devil and one of their tools was poison. This was the view of the Church, at any rate, and real witches did make use of many potions and concoctions and unguents for healing and magical purposes. Without doubt there were evil witches, who did use poison, but they were a small minority of the witch population.

The knowledge of the natural properties of plants and minerals was looked upon as a type of magic. Cornelius Agrippa (1486–1535), in his *Three Books of Occult Philosophy* (the first complete edition was published in 1533), classed it as natural magic in his threefold division of magic into natural, mathematical, and theological.

For Agrippa, natural magic was the magic inherent in herbs, stones, metals, beasts, and other aspects of the natural world. Mathematical magic was mainly concerned with astrology and numerology. The theological branch of magic dealt with angels, demons, the Hebrew names of God, and the numerical manipulation of biblical texts by means of the Jewish Kabbalah.

Ralegh would have undoubtedly been well familiar with Agrippa's book, which was the encyclopedia of magic for the Renaissance.

The confusion of classing the natural medicinal properties of herbs and stones as magical arose because it was believed that these virtues derived from the rays of the stars, and were occult in nature. The shapes, colors, and other physical properties of plants and minerals drew occult virtue from the heavens, and concentrated it in themselves, where it could be released by a wise man knowledgeable in herbal and chemical lore.

CORNELIUS AGRIPPA

No examination of the meaning of magic would be useful without Agrippa's immensely influential definition of the term, which was reused and modified and adapted for centuries. Agrippa wrote in his *Occult Philosophy* (bk. 1, ch. 2):

> Magic is a faculty of wonderful virtue, full of most high mysteries, containing the most profound contemplation of most secret things, together with the nature, power, quality, substance, and virtues thereof, as also the knowledge of whole nature, and it doth instruct us concerning the differing, and agreement of things amongst themselves, whence it produceth its wonderful effects, by uniting the virtues of things through the application of them one to the other, and to their inferior suitable subjects, joining and

knitting them together thoroughly by the powers, and virtues of the superior bodies. This is the most perfect, and chief science, that sacred, and sublimer kind of philosophy, and lastly the most absolute perfection of all most excellent philosophy.[14]

You will notice that Agrippa had nothing to say about the evils of Satan and his minions. This damned him in the eyes of the demonologists of the Christian churches. Agrippa was not ignorant of the possibility of abusing magic for evil purposes, but he did not regard magic in itself as inherently evil, as did King James and the fathers of the Church.

Astrology, which Agrippa classed as a part of mathematical magic, always inhabited a gray area. It was condemned by the more fanatical critics of the occult arts, but was nonetheless tolerated, and even encouraged, as a way of gaining foreknowledge of future events. Agrippa himself had little use for practical astrology as a way of predicting the future, but he cast charts for various rulers as a supplement to his livelihood. Similarly, John Dee drew up horoscopes for his sovereign, Queen Elizabeth the First. The rulers of Europe were a superstitious lot. They were happy to burn witches, but also eager to avail themselves of the perceived advantages of astrology.

REGINALD SCOT

The modern view of magic as a delusion and a deception began to evolve during the reign of Queen Elizabeth. In 1584 the Englishman Reginald Scot published his book *The Discoverie of Witchcraft*, in which for the first time were laid bare the tricks of itinerate stage magicians. Scot took a tolerant view of these deceptive arts (bk. 13, ch. 12):

> Manie writers have beene abused as well, by untrue reports, as by illusion, and practices of confederacie and legierdemaine, etc: sometimes imputing unto words that which resteth in the nature of the thing; and sometimes to the nature of the thing, that which proceedeth of fraud and deception of sight. But when these experiments growe to superstition or impietie, they are either to be foresaken as vaine, or denied as false. Howbeit, if these things be doone for mirth and recreation, and not to the hurt of our neighbour, nor to the abusing or prophaning of God's name, in mine opinion they are neither impious nor altogether unlawfull: though herein or hereby a naturall thing be made to seeme supernaturall. Such are the miracles wrought by jugglers, consisting in fine and nimble conveiance called legierdemaine ... [15]

While not denying the possibility of magic out of hand, Scot was quite skeptical about the powers of witches, which were the mania of his time. Even while he was writing his book, witches were being hanged and burned at the stake in England and Scotland (England hanged, Scotland burned). He wrote (bk. 1, ch. 1):

> The fables of Witchcraft have taken so fast hold and deep root in the heart of man, that fewe or none can (nowadaies) with patience indure the hand and correction of God. For if any adversitie, greefe, sicknesse,

losse of children, corne, cattell, or livertie happen unto them; by and by they exclaime uppon witches. As though there were no God in Israel that ordereth all things according to his will; punishing both just and unjust with greefs, plagues, and afflictions in maner and forme as he thinketh good: but that certaine old women heere on earth, called witches, must needs be the contrivers of all mens calamities, and as though they themselves were innocents, and had deserved no such punishments.[16]

At the time he published his book, Scot was a lone voice crying in the wilderness, but it was not long before his skeptical view became the norm, and supernatural magic in all its forms began to be regarded by scholars as wholly delusional, both on the part of those who worked it and those deceived as to its powers. This view dominated definitions of magic, and prevails at the present time. Magic began to be analyzed as an artifact of anthropology. It came to be regarded as a primitive belief that modern Westerners had cast aside, a thing of the dim past or of dark corners of the globe where savage ignorance reigned.

THE GOLDEN BOUGH

The British anthropologist Sir James Frazer (1854–1941), in his hugely influential work *The Golden Bough*, defined magic in these terms (ch. 3, sec. 1):

If we analyse the principles of thought on which magic is based, they will probably be found to resolve themselves into two: first, that like produces like, or that an effect resembles its cause; and second, that things which have once been in contact with each other continue to act on each other at a distance after the physical contact has been severed. The former principle may be called the Law of Similarity, the latter the Law of Contagion.[17]

There is never any question in Frazer's text that his readers should for a moment entertain the possibility that these magical practices may be effective. He examines the thinking process of the savage and the primitive. As a Victorian, he was quite certain that his own way of thinking was the only correct way and that soon the entire world would acknowledge its superiority. We are still waiting for that to occur, and it doesn't look as though it will happen any time soon. By far the greater part of the world continues to believe in the efficacy of magical practices, as it always has.

The first of Frazer's laws, that of similarity, indicates that there is an occult link between things of a similar nature or appearance—that is, a link in the mind of the magician may be carried outward to link in a tangible way, with magic, two similar things. What is done by the magician to one thing is expressed in the other similar thing. For example, a witch may maliciously stick a pin through the photograph of her enemy, in the expectation that her enemy will suffer pain in the part of her body where the pin has pierced the photograph.

The second of Frazer's laws, that of contagion, indicates that there is an occult link between things that have been in physical contact; that on some hidden level the contact endures, so that what is done to one thing will affect in a similar way the other thing that at one time it touched or was part of. For example, our hypothetical malevolent witch may take the hair of her enemy, and use it to stuff a small doll, which she names with the name of her enemy. Then by thrusting a pin into the doll, the enemy is injured just as if the pin had been thrust into her flesh.

So much for Frazer's laws of similarity and contagion, which are accurate as far as they go, but which do not completely define the action of magic. For example, a magician may call a spirit, and tell the spirit to injure an enemy—this action is not covered by Frazer's laws, yet it would be considered an act of magic. Frazer's laws have nothing to say about spirit invocation, Agrippa's third class of theological magic, which has always been the heart of Western magic.

As pointed out, it was believed that magic had been taught to mankind by the Watchers, fallen angels of God. This belief is not surprising, since all magic depends on the communications of spiritual beings, who tell the magician what specific things he must do in order to render his arts effective. Very few modern magicians (or witches, for that matter) comprehend this necessity, but it was universally understood and accepted, prior to the magical revival of the 18th century, that the first task of any magician working in the Western tradition was to contact a tutelary spirit or spirits.

The great grimoires are based on this assumption. They teach ways to make contact with instructing spirits. That is the primary purpose of the grimoires. After such communication has been opened, the magician learns his arts, not from books, but directly from his spiritual teachers.

This tradition of human students receiving instruction from spirit teachers has its origin in ancient shamanism. The highest teachers of the shamans are always spiritual beings. In the magical system of the Hermetic Order of the Golden Dawn, the tutelary spirit is given the title of holy guardian angel, a title derived from the grimoire known as the *Book of the Sacred Magic of Abramelin the Mage*, which gives as its highest instruction a ritual by which the magician may open communication with his or her tutelary spirit.

ALEISTER CROWLEY

After the skeptics and the anthropologists got their claws into magic, all mainstream definitions began to be prefaced with "seeming" or "pretended" of "fraudulent" or "supposed" as qualifiers. It fell to the magicians themselves to attempt to define their arts in a more sympathetic manner. The most famous definition by a modern magician is that of Aleister Crowley (1875–1947), who declared himself the Great Beast of Revelation and thought himself the herald of the Apocalypse. In the introduction to his *Magick in Theory and Practice*, he offered the definition: "Magick is the Science and Art of causing Change to occur in conformity with Will."[18]

Crowley's definition has been popular with modern magicians. It is quoted frequently, and has been modified by various authorities to suit their own interpretations, and re-presented as their own definitions of magic, sometimes with attribution to Crowley, but often without acknowledgment of his authorship. For example, Dion Fortune (1890–1946) used the definition: "Magic is the Science and Art of causing change in consciousness to occur in conformity with Will."[19]

In my opinion, Crowley's definition suffers from a couple of defects. It is too broad, for one. It covers all acts of will. Even if we make a distinction between the lower common will, and the higher magical Will, it is still too broad. The magician may use his will to fix a flat tire, and by Crowley's definition it is magic, even if the magician uses a scissor jack and a tire iron to do it.

How exactly are we to make a distinction between acts of lower will and higher Will? You might say, because the acts of higher Will are magical, but that is circular reasoning—we can only define an act as magical under Crowley's definition if we know it proceeds from the higher Will; and we can only be sure it is higher Will if it produces magical acts. The alternative is to assume that all willed acts, no matter how trivial, are magical in nature. Yet this is absurd. It makes the definition of magic so broad as to be meaningless. If all willed acts are magic, then when Crowley picked his nose, he was working the occult arts.

Another unsatisfactory aspect of Crowley's definition is the use of the term *science*. By its inherent nature, the scientific method is antipathetic to magic. The effects generated by magic are marvelous, unexpected, and beyond causal and mechanical replication. Yet science depends on the replication of data, and on the mechanical measurement of effects.

ISRAEL REGARDIE

Crowley's one-time secretary, Israel Regardie (1907–1985), wrote in his 1969 work *The Art and Meaning of Magic*: "But

I maintain, as a primal definition, that Magic whether of the Eastern or Western variety, is essentially a divine process— Theurgy, a mode of spiritual culture or development."[20]

This is an immensely important insight, which was so often missed or ignored by others attempting to define magic—that it is, at its root, always and invariably transcendent in nature. Without the transcendence of the ordinary material reality, there can be no magic. Magic is not and can never be a natural process, which is to say, a process of the natural physical world. Its transcendence is what separates magical events from natural events. It is what forever separates the occult art of magic from science. Regardie was greatly preoccupied with human psychology, and understood this transcendent communion with the divine as a psychological technique for personal evolution, but it should be understood to apply on all levels, both subjective and objective.

Regardie divided magic into three parts: "One—Divination. Two—Evocation and Vision. Three—Invocation."

Concerning the first part, he wrote: "The object of divination is quite simply, then, the construction of a psychic mechanism whereby this source of inspiration and life may be made accessible to the ordinary consciousness, to the ego."[21] The techniques of divination are magical in that they transcend ordinary consciousness and bridge the distance between the lower and higher realities, causing inspiration to flow downward with insights into common questions. In this category of magic Regardie placed geomancy (earth divination), astrology, and the Tarot.

Evocation, or the calling forth of spiritual beings, Regardie understood from a psychological perspective, as a kind

of projection of moods, phobias, and obsessions. He cited
Carl Jung (1875–1961) for his comments in the *Secret of the
Golden Flower* concerning "partial autonomous systems."
Jung remarked about this Chinese Taoist text, translated into
German by his friend Richard Wilhelm: "Being also constit-
uents of the psychic personality, they necessarily have the
character of persons. Such partial-systems appear in mental
diseases where there is no psychogenic splitting of the personality (double personality), and also, quite commonly, in
mediumistic phenomena." Regardie acknowledged that there
was an entirely different way to regard evocation. He wrote:
"This, naturally, is the subjective point of view. That there is
a purely objective occult theory I do not deny, but that cannot be dealt with here."[22] In this same category he described
scrying or astral vision by means of symbolic elemental
doorways, the tattwa symbols.

Concerning the final part of magic, Invocation, Regardie wrote: "The inevitable end of Magic is identical to
that conceived of in Mysticism, union with God-head."[23]
The practice that concerned Regardie was the invocation,
or summoning within, of a series of exalted Egyptian god
forms, with which the magician strove to achieve unity.
In this belief, Regardie echoed that of his teacher, Aleister
Crowley, who placed the invocation of the holy guardian
angel as the highest act of practical magic.

All these techniques were derived by Regardie from the
teachings of the Hermetic Order of the Golden Dawn, a Rosicrucian Society founded in London in 1888. Both Crowley
and Regardie belonged to different branches of the Golden
Dawn at different times.

Regardie made the same error as his teacher, Aleister Crowley, of attempting to link magic and science, presumably to gather to magic some of the prestige and authority that attaches in the common mind to science. He asserted, rather too strenuously, as though attempting to forestall detractors: "Magic is a scientific method. It is a valid technique. Its approach to the universe and the secret of life's meaning is a legitimate one. If it assists us to become more familiar with what we really are, it is a Science—and a most important one."[24]

Well, Regardie was wrong. Magic is not and never can be a science. However, it is an art, and has all the characteristics of art. It is intuitive and spontaneous, emotional, creative, and transcendent. It uses material substances and physical methods to capture and express transcendent realities. The canvas of magic, when worked at its highest level, is the magician himself. He becomes his own Great Work.

NEW MILLENNIUM MAGIC

In my book *New Millennium Magic*, I gave the following definition: "Magic is the art of causing transformation in the manifest universe through the universal medium of the Unmanifest."[25] The definition, which is not very catchy, not surprisingly failed to catch on. The primary point I wished to make with it is the transcendent aspect of magic. Yes, magic affects the manifest world—if it did not, we would have no awareness of it, since all that we can perceive or conceive is the manifest reality. Our thoughts and imaginings are based on sense impressions, and are thus necessarily limited by our concept of reality. But, and it is a big but... magic only works by contacting and accessing what lies beyond our normal world.

It is not merely the manipulation of things in our world. Elsewhere I wrote of magic that it captures and carries down the fire of heaven to the earth. This is merely a poetic way of saying that it applies transcendent forces to cause change in our common reality, both our inward mental reality and outward material reality (which are at root the same).

If magic were not transcendent in its action, it could be measured and replicated by science. That it has not been is a significant indication of its higher aspect. I can confidently predict that magic will never be produced by scientific procedures. Magic disdains science. From the magical perspective, science is the playground of children.

The difficulty with defining magic, positively once and forever, is that nobody really knows what magic is, not completely. We who practice it have our understanding of it, conditioned and limited by our studies and our experience, but magic goes beyond any human experience, and beyond all that has ever been written about it. It can never be captured, bottled, frozen, stuffed, or mounted. It is forever alive, forever changing its masks and its forms. Those materialists who are incapable of granting the possibility of anything higher than their tiny conceptions will never understand magic in the least degree. It is futile to even attempt to describe it to them. However, the definitions I have touched upon, limited though they must be due to the infinite and transcendent nature of magic, are useful to those of us capable of perceiving portions of its reality and its beauty.

Notes

1. Pliny, vol. 8, p. 281.

2. Ibid., p. 283.

3. Charles, p. 191.

4. Ibid., p. 192.

5. Ibid.

6. Augustine, Harvard University Press edition, vol. 7, p. 35 (William M. Green translation).

7. Augustine, Christian Literature Publishing edition, vol. 2, p. 457 (Marcus Dods translation).

8. James, p. 229.

9. Ibid., p. 230.

10. Ralegh, vol. 2, p. 379.

11. Ibid., p. 383.

12. Ibid.

13. Ibid., p. 384.

14. Agrippa, *Occult Philosophy*, p. 5.

15. Scot, p. 174.

16. Ibid., p. 1.

17. Frazer, p. 12.

18. Crowley, *Magick*, p. XII of the Introduction.

19. Ciceros, p. 70.

20. Regardie, p. 3.

21. Ibid., p. 23.

22. Ibid., p. 24.

23. Ibid., p. 29.

24. Ibid., p. 45.

25. Tyson, *New Millennium Magic*, p. 170.

2

The Magic Circle

Purpose of circles in magic

There are two opinions about the purpose for the circle in ritual magic—the first view is that it is to keep something out, and the second view is that it is to keep something in. Both are correct, and although they may seem contradictory, both views are based on the same principle—the circle is a barrier that divides inside from outside.

Take a pencil and a sheet of paper. Draw a line segment on the paper. The line seems to divide one side of the paper from the other, but it has end points, and it is possible to go around those ends—the line segment is not a true divider. However long you imagine the line to be, it is possible to imagine the paper it is on to be larger, so that the line never truly divides the plane.

Draw a circle on the sheet of paper. You will see that the division made by the circle between inside and outside is absolute. Enlarge the circle, shrink it, distort it, and it makes no difference—as long as the circle is unbroken, it creates a perfect barrier. There is no way around it.

You might argue that in our first example, we could limit the size of the imagined sheet of paper, and then it would be possible to draw a line completely across it, and divide it in an absolute sense. Yes, but to limit the size of the paper we must first draw a mental circle around it, that defines its edge. The actual physical sheet of paper is limited in just this way—its edge is its boundary circle.

What can we say about the nature of a circle, based on this little thought experiment? We can say that a circle surrounds, encloses, contains, and excludes. It defines the edge of something, and by doing so, it gives what it defines a shape. Everything we see has a circle around it. If this were not so, we would not be able to distinguish one thing from another—they would all run together and merge in our minds.

That brings up another aspect of the circle—it exists in the mind. We draw a mental circle around any thing we choose to separate from all other things. When we look at an apple tree and consider the tree as a whole, we draw a circle around the tree that divides that tree from all other trees, from the sky, the earth, from all other things that are not the tree itself; but if we choose to narrow our attention and focus it on a single apple hanging on a branch of that tree, we mentally draw a circle around that single apple.

All circles are by their inherent nature magical. They define order from chaos. There is no separation in the natural world; there are only the separations we choose to impose upon our perception of the natural world. We construct our reality piece by piece when we draw circles of identity around objects and concepts.

We are considering here the essential esoteric identity of the circle. We are not talking about just the geometric figure of the circle, although that is what is usually intended by the term. In geometry, the circle is always perfectly round. Esoterically speaking, the circle can be any shape provided that it divides outside from inside. Indeed, the circle can be no physical shape at all, but merely a concept or idea.

If you have followed this line of reasoning, you will understand that names are magic circles. This is the fabled occult power of names. When we name a thing, we separate it from everything else. It comes into discrete existence in our mind at that moment. Everything we perceive has been divided in our mind from chaos by an enclosing circle, and that circle defines the name of the thing enclosed. The subsequent process of assigning an arbitrary word-sound to the thing is secondary. We have already named it the instant we recognized its existence. That recognition makes the thing real for us—brings the thing forth into our personal reality. This is a magical act, even though it is seldom recognized as such, because it is so basic to the way our minds work.

The magic circle is usually understood in a narrower sense, as a circle drawn for the purpose of working ceremonial magic. It defines a space within which magic is facilitated. Exactly how the circle aids the working of magic has long been a matter for debate.

In traditional Western spirit evocation, the circle was used to guard the magician from the malicious actions of evil spirits, who were excluded from the circle while the magician remained safe within its boundary. In modern Wicca, the belief is that the circle retains and concentrates magical energy raised by ritual work, making it easier for the leader of the ritual to direct and release that energy for a specific desired use.

If you consider what was written above about the nature of circles in general, you can see that these two views are not incompatible. A barrier can simultaneously hold one thing out while holding another thing in. A fence around your backyard will keep your dog inside the yard, but at the same time it keeps other dogs out of the yard. The key point is that it cannot be crossed so long as it remains undivided.

The magicians of the Middle Ages and Renaissance were mostly concerned with calling up demons and spirits of a mixed type, for the performance of tasks that would have been beneath the dignity and unsuited to the nature of angels. These tasks included such work as the finding of treasure, the harming of enemies, inducing love or lust in other persons, gaining social position or power, inducing a glamour of false appearance, and so on.

By their very nature these kinds of low spirits are not inclined to help or obey human beings. Yet they are more suited for selfish tasks than the benevolent angels. The magician got around this awkwardness by calling up demons and spirits of a mixed type outside the bounds of the magic circle, while he commanded them from the safety of the space inside the circle. This protective use of the circle is unnecessary when dealing with angels of a more spiritual nature, since they never seek to do harm.

Even so, the circle was drawn for other purposes than the evocation of low spirits. Modern witches employ it to contain and concentrate the power they raise by their chanting and dancing. When the occult energy within the circle has filled the circle to such a degree that it can be felt on the surface of the skin as a kind of heat or electricity, the leader of the ritual releases it like an arrow from a bow toward its intended function.

You may ask how energy can be released from the circle, when the circle by its very nature is an unbroken barrier. This is an occult secret that until fairly recently was never explicitly revealed. I wrote about it in my first book *The New Magus*, which was published by Llewellyn Publications in 1987, and this may have been the first time the secret was clearly explained to a large number of magicians.

The circle by its nature cannot be broken and remain a circle. No point on the circumference of a circle can be singled out as an aperture without destroying the integrity of the circle, since all points must remain undifferentiated and undivided if the circle is to stay whole. The only way in or out of a circle is through the single point at its center, which by the very nature of a circle is defined. Yet all points within the area of a circle are the same—one mathematical point does not differ from another mathematical point by its nature, but only by its position.

The center is relative. Any point in space that the human mind chooses to make its viewpoint becomes the center of the universe for that viewing consciousness. We think of ourselves as looking outward through our eyes from some point within our skulls, but this is arbitrary. We can just as easily regard the world from the tip of our right index finger, or from the cat lying on the fireplace hearth across the room.

The practical consequence from a magical standpoint, with regard to the circle, is that any point within the circumference of a circle (but no point on the circumference) can be regarded by the magician as its center point and used as an aperture in or out of that circle.

When the high priestess of a Wiccan coven releases from the circle the accumulated occult energy of a ritual to the fulfillment, she does so by opening the point doorway at the center of the circle. This happens even if she is unaware of what she is doing. There is only one way in or out of the circle, so to release the pent-up energy, the high priestess must open the center—that particular point within the circle that she chooses, by the focus of her will, to represent the center point of the circle.

Points are opened by expanding them. The expansion of a point is accomplished by means of a spiral. Only spiral energy can move through a point. Wiccans raise what is known as a cone of power within the circle. The cone has a spiral energy and it focuses upon a point, which is the center point of the circle. It is through this expanded point that the concentrated energy of the ritual is released, to fly like an arrow to its target, where it accomplishes its purpose.

Necromancers working with demons from within a protective magic circle sometimes pierce the circle with a sword to manipulate objects, or to compel obedience from the demons they have evoked outside the circle. They seem to pierce the side of the circle with the blade of the sword. Probably they themselves believed that they were piercing the side of the circle when they extended the steel blade beyond its boundary.

This is not the case. As already explained, a circle only remains a circle for so long as it is unbroken, and were it broken even for an instant, its protective power would cease. No, the blade of the sword actually extends through the point chosen by the necromancer as the center of the circle. This occurs on the subconscious level. By choosing a place to project the sword blade, the necromancer defines the center point, distinguishing it from all other points within the circle, and by projecting the blade he opens that point with spiral energy.

CIRCLES OF STONE AND DANCING RINGS

Mention magic circles to the average person, and the first thing he will think of is Stonehenge. The sheer beauty and mystery of that ancient ring of standing stones on the Salisbury Plain has so captured the modern mind that it has become iconic. Yet it is far from unique. Similar stone rings of widely varying sizes and degrees of sophistication are to be found not only across Britain, or even across Europe, but throughout the entire world. The most ancient that have been discovered to date are probably the rings of curious T-shaped standing stones that have recently been unearthed in southern Turkey.

The place is called Göbekli Tepe. It is near the city of San-liurfa (formerly known as Edessa), which lies around ten miles to its west. The unique T-stones were discovered in 1994 by a Kurdish shepherd, who happened to notice some curiously regular stone blocks poking up from the ground while tending his flock. What he discovered has been called the greatest archaeology find in history.

The stone circles excavated from under their covering of earth are 12,000 years old—7,000 years older than Stonehenge. There are an estimated twenty rings of stones, although only four have been completely excavated to date. Most of the stones are about eight feet tall, but one has been found in a nearby quarry that is twenty-eight feet long, so much larger stones may wait to be uncovered.

The discovery at Göbekli Tepe shows that human beings were building elaborate complexes of stone circles even before they began to settle in villages and farm the land. That is how important the making of circles was to these early cultures. Undoubtedly they were used for religious rituals, but for ancient man there was no clear separation between religion and magic. Shamanism is an almost perfect blending of the two. The shaman is both priest and magician.

Some researchers have contended that these stone circles were built to mark the windings of the stars and planets in the heavens—as a sort of elaborate form of sundial. But if this were their only function, or even their primary function, it could have been accomplished just as well with much less massive or elaborate constructions. Imagine how much labor went into the construction of Stonehenge, or Göbekli Tepe.

No, the circles of stones served a magical purpose that was of the highest possible significance. They defined a sacred space, concentrated ritual energies within that space, and protected it from defilement by disharmonious forces. The maintenance of these sacred spaces must have been more important to the peoples who built these great stone rings than any other purpose in their lives. They devoted generations to building them. The only comparable act of devotion in historical times was the construction of the great cathedrals of Europe, which took centuries to complete.

A ring of standing stones defines a permanent circle to sanctify and empower a specific spot on the surface of the earth, but magic rings of an impermanent kind were also constructed for ritual purposes. The most ephemeral form of magic circle was that formed by the bodies of dancing witches, or the seated ring of chanting shamans. This sort of magic circle could be formed anywhere a nomadic tribe stopped for the night, and although its locality was always different, its manner of formation was always the same, and lent the ritual practice a continuity that persisted in spite of the ceaselessly changing landscape.

We can catch a faint echo of this kind of nomadic ritual practice in the books of the Old Testament that describe the early Hebrews wandering in the desert. Each night they erected a tent to house the Ark of the Covenant. The walls of the tent became the magic circle that contained the occult power of the Ark, and also excluded those who were considered unfit to approach the Ark.

Still more primitive nomadic peoples could accomplish the same ends without a tent, by defining the magic circle with their own tribesmen gathered into a ring. At its center a fire was probably maintained, and around this fire a shaman danced and sang to raise occult power. By dancing around the fire, the center point of the circle was opened, and the energy released to fulfill its function.

European witchcraft descended from shamanism. This is self-evident—there are too many parallels between shamanism and witchcraft to reach any other conclusion. Although we can only conjecture as to how primitive nomadic tribes must have formed their magic circles, we have a much clearer idea how the witches of the Middle Ages went about it. The practices of witches are described in the transcripts of the European witch trials.

These court records are to be viewed with the utmost skepticism. The confessions of witches were extracted under torture, or the threat of torture, and accused individuals tried to tell their captors exactly what they wanted to hear. Even so, the general consistency in the descriptions suggests that they are based upon some collective cultic activity—that there were indeed witches and that they did indeed gather for the practice of magic and for worship.

This was the conclusion of Margaret A. Murray in her highly controversial yet influential book *The Witch-Cult in Western Europe*. Murray's findings have been dismissed by most mainstream anthropologists, yet her central contention, that the mythology of witchcraft represents an echo of a surviving pagan religion, or at least a kind of cultic set of magical practices with religious elements, is plausible based on the detail and consistency of the confessions of those interrogated as witches.

We read in the testimony of accused witches that they gathered at their sabbats to perform works of magic and worship. Those recording these matters were Christian priests, so naturally in the transcripts of the witch trials, the works of magic are invariably supposed to have been evil and the worship always assumed to have been devil worship. Yet we have only the assertions of the Christian priests that this was the case. It seems more likely that the magic worked by witches at their gatherings was of a mixed nature.

Witches danced in a circle at their gatherings. This was known as the round dance or ring dance. Margaret A. Murray wrote of it in her 1931 book *The God of the Witches*:

> The ring dance was specially connected with the fairies, who were reported to move in a ring holding hands. It is the earliest known dance, for there is a representation of one at Cogul in north-eastern Spain (Catalonia), which dates to the Late Palaeolithic or Capsian period. The dancers are all women, and their peaked hoods, long breasts, and elf-locks should be noted and compared with the pictures and descriptions of elves and fairies. They are apparently dancing round a small male figure who stands in the middle. A similar dance was performed and represented several thousand years later, with Robin Goodfellow in the centre of the ring and his worshippers forming a moving circle round him.[1]

Concerning the ring dance of witches, J. M. McPherson wrote in his 1929 book *Primitive Beliefs in the North-East of Scotland*:

> The ring dance usually took place round some object. Thomas Leyis with a great number of other witches "came to the Market and Fish Cross of Aberdeen, under the conduct and guidance of the devil present with you, all in company, playing before you on his kind of instruments, ye all danced about the said

Cross, the said Thomas was foremost and led the ring." These danced round the Cross. Margaret Og was charged with going to Craigleauch "on Halloween last, and there accompanied by thy own two daughters and certain others, ye all danced together about a great stone under the conduct of Satan, your master, a long space." Here the stone was the centre round which they danced.[2]

Discounting the slanders of the Church inquisitors concerning the presence of Satan in the gatherings of witches, we can see in these ring dances the formation of a kind of dynamic, moveable magic circle. As is the case with modern witchcraft covens when they form a circle for ritual purposes, the center of the ring had a focus for its concentrated energies. Usually this was the leader of the ritual, but the dances might also take place around a standing stone, altar, or other object of power. The rotation of the dancers provided the spiral energy needed to focus upon the center of the circle.

The close correspondence between the ring dance of witches and the ring dance of fairies is part of the whole complex of strong ties that exist between the lore of witches and the lore of fairies. Fairy rings, naturally occurring circles that appeared in the grass of meadows and in woods, are the result of the growth of fungus under the surface of the ground, but they were thought to be made by fairies dancing with their hands joined. Other names for these circular phenomena were sorcerers' rings (French: *ronds de sorciers*) or witches' rings (German: *Hexenringe*). By some rural folk they were thought to be formed when witches gathered at their sabbats to dance.

European witches met out of doors, under the moon and stars, and gathered in grassy meadows on in clearings in the forest. They danced on the ground, which was unmarked with symbolic patterns, forming the patterns of their rituals with their own bodies and with their movements. It shows how important the circle is for magical practice, that even under these conditions witches felt a need to define a circle with their dance.

MAGIC CIRCLES IN THE GRIMOIRES

The round dance of witches is perhaps the purest form of magic circle. European magicians did not have the option of using a dozen human beings with linked hands to form a circle. They worked alone, or with one or two assistants, and usually performed their rituals beneath a roof on a floor of stone or wood. It was the usual practice to draw or inscribe a magic circle on the floor of the chamber of practice prior to beginning the ritual, using charcoal or chalk. There were other methods for defining the circle—it could be laid down in the form of joined strips of fur or skin, or defined by a rope laid out on the floor, or even painted upon a canvas or rug that was unfolded across the floor— but the usual way was to draw or inscribe the circle.

The term *circle* is used here in its occult, not its mathematical, sense. Ritual circles were seldom perfectly circular, or simple in nature. They consisted of concentric circles within a square, or multiple circles, or more involved geometric patterns such as pentagrams, hexagrams, or octagrams. These complex patterns on the floor of the ritual chamber are still magic circles, in that they were used to divide inside from outside with a continuous and unbroken line or set of lines.

One of the oldest of the grimoires, and the most authoritative, *The Key of Solomon the King*, describes the making of a complex circle. It is evident from its size and manner of formation that this circle is to be made out of doors on the ground.

The magician takes a cord nine feet in length and uses a sword to fix one end to the center of the working space. With the cord pulled taunt, he uses the other end to inscribe with a knife the line of a circle on the ground that is eighteen feet in diameter. A cross is drawn through the center of the circle to divide it into four quadrants—east, west, south, and north. Into each quadrant is placed the symbol of that direction of space.

This is the actual magic circle—the magical barrier that protects the magician. Beyond this initial circle, which is called the Circle of Art, other elaborations are to be inscribed that are part of the compound magic circle but not its essential core. Three more concentric circles are to be drawn, each one foot larger in radius than the initial circle, so that three bands are formed by the four circles. Within the outermost of these circular bands, pentagrams are to be inscribed, along with the names and symbols of God.

A square is drawn outside these three bands, or four circles, and outside the square a larger square, so that the corners of the smaller square touch the midpoints of the sides of the larger square. The squares are to be oriented so that the corners of the larger square point in the four directions—east and west, north and south.

It should be noted that the illustration in S. L. MacGregor Mathers' edition of the *Key of Solomon* (figure 81) does not match the description of how to make the circle (which occurs in book 2, chapter 9 of that work). The confusion arises with regard to the concentric circles—how many there are to be, what is to be put in them, and where it is to be put. The illustration in Mathers' book shows only three circles, not the four described. I will quote the relevant passage of text from Mathers' edition, then explain where the confusion arises. The numbering within the square brackets is mine and has been used for the sake of clarity.

Then within the Circle mark our four regions, namely, towards the East, West, South, and North, wherein place Symbols; and beyond the limits of this Circle [1] describe with the Consecrated Knife or Sword another Circle [2], but leaving an open space therein towards the North whereby thou mayest enter and depart beyond the Circle of Art. Beyond this again thou shalt describe another Circle [3] at a foot distance with the aforesaid Instrument, yet ever leaving therein an open space for entrance and egress corresponding to the open space already left in the other. Beyond this again make another Circle [4] at another foot distance, and beyond these two Circles [2 and 3], which are beyond the Circle of Art [1] yet upon the same Centre, thou shalt describe Pentagrams with the Symbols and Names of the Creator therein so that they may surround the Circle already described.[3]

The first circle with a radius of nine feet is the Circle of Art. The second concentric circle has a radius of ten feet, the third concentric circle a radius of eleven feet, and the fourth concentric circle a radius of twelve feet. A gap is left in the north of each circle for the entrance of the magician after he has finished completing the drawing of the pattern. The magician closes the gap once he stands inside. This gap is not mentioned explicitly for the innermost and outermost circles, but it is implied. In some of the older illustrations of magic circles, this gap in the north appears to be a permanent part of the circle—a kind of corridor for entry and exits.[4]

The text seems to indicate that the pentagrams are to be drawn within the outermost of the three bands, between circles 3 and 4. It is not specified how many pentagrams are to be used, but Mathers' diagram shows four. However, in the diagram they are located upon the square that surrounds the four circles, not within the outermost band of those circles. Based on the text, these pentagrams should be placed between circles 3 and 4, along with divine names, so that the band of pentagrams and divine names surrounds the inner circles. The text seems to imply that the divine names should be written within the pentagrams, but I believe this is misleading—the names should probably be written within the outermost band of the circles, between circles 3 and 4, beside the pentagrams. A pentagram should be located between divine names. The "symbols" of the Creator may be the four Hebrew letters of Tetragrammaton, IHVH.

There is no indication in the text what names are to be written within the bands of the circles, apart from the outermost, which does not even appear on Mathers' diagram. The diagram shows in the innermost band the Hebrew divine names (which I have transcribed here into Latin characters) AVIAL, ADNI, IHVH, and TzBAVTh. The second band contains the words MI KMKH BALIM IHVH. These are the only Hebrew words shown on Mathers' diagram.

The vast size alone of this complex magic circle would make it all but unusable. The smallest part of it, the Circle of Art, is a full eighteen feet in diameter. The size of the larger square outside the concentric circles is around twice that width. To draw this circle indoors would require a room some thirty-two feet across, at least, in its smallest dimension. Many modern houses are not this wide.

Fortunately for magicians, the circle in the *Key of Solomon* is only one such design that may be used. At the opposite size extreme, some older woodcuts show the magician working within a circle so tiny, it is barely large enough to contain him. A few of these older illustrations even show the demons evoked into the circle while the magician stands outside it unprotected, but this is contrary to the usual use of the circle and should probably be considered an error. Malicious spirits are evoked outside the Circle of Art, usually into a triangle, but sometimes within a smaller circle with the magician safely within the larger circle. As is stated in the *Key of Solomon*, he who works within the Circle of Art "shall be at safety as within a fortified Castle, and nothing shall be able to harm him."[5]

DRAWING THE PHYSICAL CIRCLE

Do not be alarmed if you cannot make out the letters of all the obscure names in the magic circles of the grimoires.

Some illustrations of these circles are so corrupt, it would take a Solomon risen from the grave to decipher them. The Hebrew and Greek characters have devolved into nothing more than meaningless squiggles. Happily for the modern magician, there are an infinite number of possible patterns for the magic circle, and all of them will work effectively provided the magician who creates them follows a few basic principles, which I propose to give you. A circle you design yourself, if it is rightly designed, will always be more effective than a circle you copy out of an old book.

The first consideration of a magic circle is that it must be an unbroken line the end of which joins up with its beginning. It does not necessarily need to be perfectly circular in shape, although rightly made circles will usually contain at their root a single unbroken circle, beneath whatever elaborations have been added. Bear this in mind—base your magic circle on a simple, unbroken ring, and it will serve you well. It should be made as large as necessary so that you can work comfortably within it. A traditional size is nine feet in diameter, but for a single person working without an altar, a circle as small as six feet across will be fine. If you can make the circle nine feet across, you will be able to set an altar at its center, and you will have enough room to move around it.

The world is usually divided into four directions or quarters. The magic circle is similarly divided into four quadrants by lines extending to the north, east, south, and west. It is not essential to physically mark these quarters of the circle, but you should be aware of this division, which is the most fundamental division of the magic circle. The magic altar is often placed at the center of the circle, and the altar has a square top with four sides. Each of its four sides should face one of the four directions. The room in which the magic circle will usually be constructed will likely have four walls. Again, these walls may be referred to the four directions and four quarters of the world. The wall that is closest to the east can be used for the direction of east; the wall closest to the south can be used for the direction of south; and so on. Align the sides of your altar with the walls of the room.

The divine names that are generally used to act as guardians of the circle are four in number, one name for each quarter of space. It does not matter which specific divine names you choose. The grimoires generally use Hebrew names of God culled from the Bible, either written out in Hebrew characters, or in Greek or Latin characters. IHVH, Adonai, Eheieh, and Elohim are serviceable. You do not need to use divine names from the Bible if you have an aversion to conventional religions. Pagan divine names will serve equally well, provided that they are names or titles of the supreme god of the pagan pantheon with which you are working. If you were to use classical Greek mythology for your pantheon, you would choose four names for Zeus. If you were to use the Nordic pantheon, you would choose four names for Odin, or Woden. You will find that supreme gods always have a multitude of names and titles from which to choose.

These four divine names are applied to your inner circle, the root of your magic circle, which is called in the *Key of Solomon* the Circle of Art. Draw a second circle outside the first, so that there is from six inches to a foot of distance between them, and mark the names in this ring. They are your strongest final line of defense, your ultimate authority by which you command spirits of a malicious or mixed nature. Like the greatest artillery, they are powerful but not versatile.

Outside this first ring you should construct a second ring by drawing a third, larger circle, in which you should place the names of four lesser gods, or if you are working with the Jewish or Christian systems, the names of the four archangels, Michael, Raphael, Gabriel, and Uriel. Each lesser god, or archangel, should be chosen to serve as the active arm of the divine name to which it corresponds. The archangel executes the will of God that is defined by the divine name of that quarter. It is the extension or projection of that power.

All the names should be written to be read from outside the circle, not from inside. This important detail is usually overlooked in the grimoires. It is the spirits beyond the boundary of the circle who will be barred from entry by the power of the names, so the names are written for their benefit.

A third line of defense should consist of a third ring, defined by a fourth larger circle, in which are inscribed four names of lesser or earthly spirits that are under the authority of the archangels or lesser gods of the second circle. These earthly spirits will execute minor and mundane tasks assigned to them by the archangels of the four quarters. In traditional Western Judeo-Christian magic, there are four elemental kings that may be used for this purpose: Djin, Nichsa, Paralda, and Ghob. Sometimes the nature of the archangels is too elevated to effectively deal with material concerns, and when this is the case these earthly spirits act as their arms, just as the archangels act as the arms of the divine names.

If you have followed this division, you will now have three rings defined by four circles, each ring with four names written in it, one name for each quarter of the world. You may place whatever elaborations you will outside these circles, but the basic circle has already been made and will serve any purpose to which it is put.

I'll give the Golden Dawn arrangement for the four sets of divine, archangelic, and kingly names on the quarters, just as a reference. Other names may be used with equally good results.

East: IHVH—Raphael—Paralda
South: Adonai—Michael—Djin
West: Eheieh—Gabriel—Nichsa
North: AGLA—Uriel—Ghob

An attractive elaboration you can use, if you have sufficient space, is to draw a heptagram outside the outermost circle so that the circles fit within its open center. The form of the heptagram that has a line which reflects from every second point has a large space at its center. The names of the seven planetary angels can then be written at the bases of each of the seven triangles that form the points of this heptagram. This circle is excellent for planetary magic.

The question of what to use to mark the magic circle on the floor always arises. In past centuries a piece of charcoal from the fire was used, or sometimes a piece of chalk. Floors were usually rough boards in those times, or flagstones. Charcoal or chalk do not work well on a modern carpet, or even on polished hardwood.

A popular method is to lay out the circle with colored tape. This can be bought at any craft store. You can be conservative and use white tape for the entire circle, or if you wish, you can differentiate the fourfold division of the circle by using tapes that are colored the four elemental colors. The Golden Dawn correspondence of colors for the four directions would be: east—yellow, south—red, west—blue, north—black (or green).

Projecting the astral circle

Now I must tell you the most important part of casting a magic circle. What you have just made on the floor of your ritual chamber—this elaborate construction of three rings with its divine, angelic, and elemental kingly names—is not a magic circle. It is only the physical husk or shell of a magic circle. It has no life, no reality on the astral level, until you infuse life into it, and make it real.

It is for this reason—because the circle you have drawn or laid out on your floor is a dead thing—that I have not written about making a gap in the north to enter the circle. The circle does not exist until you empower it, so making a gap in the north is not necessary. You may just step across the edge of the physical circle to enter it.

To empower and bring the circle to life, it must be projected or cast on the astral level. This is done in the imagination, by a process of successive visualization, at the start of your rituals. The circle you envision on the astral plane will not correspond in every respect to the circle you have drawn on the floor, any more than the astral temple you have erected in your mind will match exactly your physical workspace.

To cast the circle on the astral level, you stand within the physical circle, visualizing yourself standing in the astral temple you have built up in your imagination, and then mentally walk around the inner edge of the physical circle, projecting the astral circle above it with astral fire so that it floats in the air at the level of your heart. If your physical circle is small, it is sufficient to turn on your own axis while projecting the astral circle in the air at heart level.

After you have projected the astral circle, you must sustain it in your imagination for the remainder of the ritual. It is not an empty exercise—when you make the astral circle, it remains in existence in your mind. The more clearly you can visualize it, the more potent its working. Never step through the astral circle once it has been projected.

The astral circle is projected from the right hand, the side of the body that projects. The right side is projective, the left side receptive. You can use an instrument such as a wand to project the circle, or your right index finger. If you use your finger, it is good to have a magic ring on that finger, the better to channel your energies. The astral fire of the circle is drawn out of your heart center and ejected from your wand, or index finger, in a continuous stream, as though it were a stream of burning liquid.

You can visualize this fire to be of any color, but a glowing yellow-white flame is neutral in a magical sense and will serve for most ritual purposes.

I have developed a very specific way of projecting occult energies. I lay my left palm flat over my heart-center at a comfortable angle, as though taking a pledge, and extend my right index finger. I then visualize astral fire shining from my heart-center the way light shines from a flame. I draw this fire out of my heart-center through the palm of my left hand, up my left arm, across my shoulders, and then project it strongly down my right arm and out through my right index finger. The astral fire traces an expanding spiral course through my body.

After projecting the magic circle on the astral level, you should invoke the names of the gods, archangels, and kings by turning to face their directions successively, or by walking around the circle to stand in their quarters successively. Start in the east and turn sunwise. Call forth the power of IHVH in the east, then Adonai in the south, Eheieh in the west, and AGLA in the north. Return to the east and invoke the archangel of the east, Raphael, then go to the south and invoke Michael, then Gabriel in the west, and Uriel in the north. Return east and invoke the king Paralda, then the king Djin in the south, the king Nichsa in the west, and the king Ghob in the north. Return to your starting place in the east, or face east if you are turning on your own axis within a small circle.

In this way you will have gone around the circle three times, once for the names of God, once for the names of the archangels, and once for the names of the kings. This turning creates a whirl or tourbillion—a kind of occult vortex—that draws down magical power into the circle and fills it with astral light. If you have done the invocation rightly, you will see this light strongly glowing in your visualized astral circle, and you may even see it in the physical circle, glowing on the air with a soft radiance.

You have in this way cast the circle and energized it. You are ready for whatever ritual work you intend to perform.

Breaking the circle

When that work is finished, you must deliberately break the ring of the astral circle before you leave the physical circle. I say again, do not walk through the astral circle. Nothing so terrible will happen if you do, but by walking through it you demonstrate that it lacks substance. This is not a good practice. You want to make the astral circle so real, so tangible, that it would be physically impossible for you to walk through it without first breaking it.

Before breaking the astral circle, banish the four regions of space that lie beyond its barrier. By the authority of the God names of those quarters, command any spirits who may be lingering there to depart in peace. Do this in a quiet but resolute voice, or if you are performing a silent mental ritual, with firmly focused thoughts that are subvocalized in your throat. Pay attention to how the air of the ritual chamber feels after you banish the quarters. Does it feel calm and empty? Or does it have a waiting, watchful feeling? If it does not feel empty, perform the banishing a second time, or even a third time, with greater emphasis.

After the four quarters have been banished, it is safe to break the astral circle. When you have divided the circle with your will, you may draw it back into your heart-center by reversing the steps with which you projected it. Break it in the east (that is the usual starting point used by most magicians, although I start my rituals in the south). Draw it into yourself by walking around it widdershins if it is a large circle, or by turning widdershins if it is a small circle. Draw it back into your heart through your extended left index finger, the side of reception.

RING, SASH, AND CIRCLET

Various articles are worn by the ceremonial magician that are in themselves magic circles that enclose and protect the body, by which different forms of occult force may be concentrated or projected.

The magic finger ring is a standard article for traditional Western magicians. It is customary for a familiar spirit to be bound to the ring, so that the spirit lends its power to the ring, and may be called forth from the ring at need to perform services for the magician. A magic ring worn on the finger is described in the *Key of Solomon*, showing how ancient this instrument must have been. The Greek writer Philostratus described magic rings worn by the sage and magician Apollonius of Tyana, who lived around the time of Jesus, and the use of magic rings must have been old even in the time of Apollonius. Cornelius Agrippa was supposed to have worn such a ring.

In addition to serving as the receptacle for a familiar spirit, the ring is used to project power through the finger on which it is worn. Usually this is the right index finger, the most willful and potent finger for projection. As energy runs around the circle of the ring, forming a vortex of power, it is directed out through the point gateway at the center of the magic circle defined by the ring, and channeled along the axis defined by the extended finger.

Another magic circle worn on the body is the sash. This is usually wrapped three times around the waist of the magician and tied, although sometimes the sash is closed by a fastener in the shape of a serpent biting its own tail, so that the sash forms a symbolic ouroboros. The sash is sometimes made from seven bands of colored fabric or ribbon that are the seven colors of the rainbow and correspond with the seven planets of traditional magic. The sash I use is made of seven braided cords, each cord dyed one of the rainbow colors. Modern witches have their own version of the sash called the cord.

The function of the sash is manifold, but one purpose is to contain and concentrate vitality within the center of the magician's body. It also offers protection against possession attempts or other intrusions into the body by spirits. Different sashes sometimes form marks of rank within occult orders, just as different colored belts are ranks in the martial arts.

The third magic circle often worn on the body by Western magicians is the circlet, a band of metal worn around the head. Mine is in the shape of a serpent swallowing its tail and is fashioned from copper. Silver and gold will also serve for making the circlet.

The circlet concentrates occult energy in the head, the seat of the will and the reason. It has the function of strengthening and focusing the mind. Its physical pressure on the forehead helps to awaken and open the ajna chakra, the third eye, which is located between the eyebrows. The circlet is helpful during scrying for this reason.

CONCLUSION

There is no aspect of ritual occultism more ancient or more essential than the magic circle. Indeed, it is difficult to find systems of magic that do not use the circle in some form, and when they are found, they seem incomplete and naked without it. The magic circle is older than Solomon, older than Moses, and occurs throughout the world in all religions and systems of witchcraft and thaumaturgy. It divides, excludes, protects, attracts, focuses, and concentrates, as these functions are needed by the magician. It is used not merely for evocations, but for invocations, for charging of talismans, for scrying, for projecting accumulated occult energy, and even for meditation. A correct understanding of the circle, not only how to project it, but what it signifies symbolically, is the most basic knowledge any magician can possess, and no magician can be said to know anything of importance about magic who has not mastered the use of the circle.

NOTES

1. Murray, *God of the Witches*, pp. 109–110.

2. McPherson, p. 169.

3. Mathers, *Key of Solomon*, p. 99.

4. Skinner and Rankine, p. 70.

5. Mathers, *Key of Solomon*, p. 100.

3

The Nature of Spirits

For the past decade and longer, no questions in the field of esoteric studies and practices have fascinated me more than those dealing with the nature of spiritual beings. What are they? Where do they come from? Where do they go when we cease to perceive them? How much power do they possess, and what types of power? Why do they bother interacting with human beings? How do they communicate and reveal themselves to us? Are they independent of the individual human mind, or a part of it? Can they transcend the physical separation between one mind and another? What is the relationship between spirit apparitions and dreams? Are there many kinds of spirits, or only one spirit essence that presents itself in different masks? Are we spirits?

The answers to these and similar questions are elusive. This is obvious from the lack of historical consensus about spirits, despite the continuing presence of spirits in the human world since the dawn of history. Every culture has its own ideas about spiritual beings. Many believe that spirits are the surviving personalities of dead humans. Some regard spirits as the individuated expressions of the universal life force of nature, present in trees and springs and mountains. Others look upon them as potent divine beings responsible for the creation and shepherding of the human race. In modern times a new theory has popped up, that these beings are intelligent life forms from other star systems. Biologists have dismissed spiritual creatures as aberrations in the working of the brain; psychologists, as creations of the imagination.

The question of what spirits are is made more confusing by the multiplicity of spirit types. If we list some of the kinds of spiritual beings that have been observed in our own Western culture, it is easy to see why no common consensus exists as to the fundamental nature of all spirits:

Divine	Celestial	Terrestrial	Infernal	Human
creators	solar	earthy	destroyers	ghosts
messengers	lunar	watery	liars	ancestor spirits
teachers	planetary	airy	confusers	poltergeists
watchers	stellar	fiery	concealers	vampires
enforcers	ethereal	natural	punishers	shapeshifters
protectors	portentous	familiar	tempters	doppelgangers

This table is by no means intended as complete. Each entry can be subdivided into numerous classes of spirit, and additional entries might be added. Divine spirits roughly break down into gods and angels, but there are numerous kinds of gods and groups of angels. In monotheistic religions such as Christianity only one god is recognized, relegating all the other lesser gods to the class of angels. These helpers of God have numerous functions. They assist in creation; carry messages from heaven to earth, and from earth to heaven; instruct human beings in sacred matters; observe the events transpiring on the earth; enforce the will of God; and offer protection to certain individuals, families, or groups.

Celestial spirits, which are spirits associated with the heavens, are primarily linked with either the stars or the planets. In astrology the sun and moon are termed planets, but this is not strictly accurate, and in any case these orbs of the heavens are important enough to be considered apart from the rest of the wandering bodies of the sky. Ethereal spirits are those associated with the "spaces between the stars," to use the words of H. P. Lovecraft. The fifth occult element, ether, was thought until the last 150 years or so to pervade the universe and to fill up the space between the stars. Portentous spirits are those attached to heavenly portents, such as comets or meteors. It was believed that every celestial event had its own resident intelligence.

Terrestrial spirits may usually be classed either as pure elementals or as spirits of nature. Elementals are of four types: spirits of fire known as Salamanders, spirits of water known as Undines, spirits of air known as Sylphs, and spirits of earth known as Gnomes. This system was created by the German magician Paracelsus (1493–1541) to classify the spiritual beings of the earthly sphere. The division is artificial, since there is no such thing as a completely pure element in nature. Elementals are spirits that overwhelmingly predominate in one elemental quality or another. By contrast, nature spirits are often a mixture of elemental qualities, just as human beings are. These are the creatures of ancient mythology and folklore, said to populate the wild places of the earth. Some of the spirits of our elemental sphere deliberately choose to associate with human beings. These are the familiars that accompany and assist magicians and witches.

The infernal spirits are a distorted mirror inversion of the heavenly spirits, as we might expect from the myth of the fall of the angels. Before their fall, the angels that fought beside the rebel Lucifer were of the same type as the angels that fought alongside Michael, the champion of God. But the fall into the abyss caused their noble qualities to become corrupted. Demons are corrupted angels, at least in the view of Christian theology. The creator angels are mirrored by the destroyer demons. The messengers of truth are mirrored by the spreaders of lies. And so on for the rest. There are more types than I have listed, but to some extent these divisions are theoretical and arbitrary. Early Christian theologians constructed an elaborate hierarchy of hell that was the exact inversion of the hierarchy of heaven.

Finally, there are spiritual beings thought to be based on the human soul, either while still living or after death. Some of the more important types are listed in the table. Ghosts are generally believed to be the actual souls of the dead that have somehow become trapped in the earthly sphere. Many religions around the world are based on the concept of ancestor spirits—the souls of the dead who either voluntarily or involuntarily have remained on earth in communication with their descendants. Vodoun is at its root an ancestor religion. The great gods of Vodoun began as the powerful souls of the dead, who were venerated by their descendants. Poltergeists and doppelgangers are spirits projected from those still living. Poltergeists arise from, or are drawn to, adolescents; doppelgangers are spectral images of the living thought to foreshadow their deaths. Spiritual vampires are believed by some to be either the surviving remnants of departed humans, that consume the life force of the living, or projections of living human beings who draw nourishment from others by occult means. Shapeshifters such as werewolves are sometimes astral projections of those asleep. Both vampires and werewolves have become materialized in popular culture, but they began as spirit manifestations. They are both types of the hungry ghost.

There is no pretense of completeness in this table, but it illustrates the diversity of spiritual beings. No wonder it is difficult to isolate the factors that spirits share in common. Additional confusion is added by the tendency to conceive spirits as material. Gods, angels, demons, vampires, werewolves—all were given physical bodies in folklore. This was even true of ghosts in ancient Egypt. What, then, are some of the things that can be said about the nature of spirits that transcend their superficial differentiations?

SPIRITS APPEAR TO BE PHYSICAL

When spirits are seen or otherwise perceived by humans, they are assumed to be present in the material world. Those who look upon them believe the spirits they see are standing in front of them. This is what their sense of sight reports, so we can hardly blame them for committing this error. Sometimes the bodies of spirits appear translucent or shift and change before the sight. At other times they can be seen to speak but cannot be heard; or they can be felt but not seen;

or heard but neither seen nor felt. However, because our perception of spirits is sensory, the assumption is usually made that spirits are physical in one way or another. This is why aspiring paranormal investigators attempt to record spirit voices or try to take photographs of ghosts—they are operating from the underlying assumption that spirits are physical, even if their bodies are composed of some unknown and rarified substance.

SPIRITS ARE NEVER PHYSICAL

Contrary to this almost universal belief in the physical reality of spirits, my own experience and study have shown that spirits are never physical, in the way that the objects around us are physical. A chair and an angel may appear to occupy the same dimension of space when the angel sits in the chair, but actually they are on two completely separate planes of reality. Even though the angel we sit chatting with appears to be present in front of us, it is not. Or at least, not in the usual sense. Spirits, no matter what their type, are always projections from the unconscious mind. I am not implying that spirits are mere fantasies, or that they are productions of the individual human mind, only that they communicate by projecting their images, words, touches, and so on, from the unconscious part of the human mind into the conscious part.

For this projection, they employ what I have called sensory metaphors (see the separate essay on this subject: "Sensory Metaphors," chapter 8). These metaphors resemble sense impressions of physical objects but are really spirit communications masquerading as ordinary sense impressions. We cannot perceive spirits directly, so spirits manipulate human senses in order to appear to be physical beings. In this way they can communicate and interact with us through our seeing, hearing, feeling, smelling, and tasting. A sensory metaphor is a substitution for a sense impression, a translation of something we could not perceive into something we can perceive.

Consciousness can only comprehend what is based on the five physical senses. Even our dreams and fantasies are cast in terms of sense impressions. What lies beyond the senses cannot be known by human intelligence. The lower mind is simply not equipped to handle it. Spirits dwell beyond the senses, and in order to make themselves known, they pretend to be beings susceptible to sense perception.

The practical consequence is that although spirits are not in any way physical beings, they always appear to be physical beings, and more than this, they always must appear to be physical beings or we would never be able to perceive them in any way. This explains how angels have come to men and women in what seemed to be completely normal, living human bodies. So great is the control over human senses by angels that they can perfectly simulate a material existence on all five channels of sense. They can be touched, heard, seen, smelled, and tasted. Sometimes they make love to human beings, an act that in its completeness requires all five senses to be active.

When I write of spirits manipulating the senses, I do not mean that they stimulate the actual physical sense organs. These are bypassed entirely. For example, the eyes play no role whatsoever when we see a spirit. The sensory metaphors used by spirits to communicate with us are implanted directly into the brain, and to our perceptions appear to be projected onto the greater world, the way a motion picture image is projected onto a theater screen. We seem to see a spirit standing before us, but what we actually experience is a mental construct manufactured by the spirit and implanted directly into our brain for the purpose of communication and interaction.

Not all spirits have such perfect and complete control over human sensory impressions as do angels. Some are able to manipulate only one sense, or two senses, and even then the control is imperfect. The result is a silent, translucent image, or a figure that has no color, or a disembodied voice, or a ghostly touch. And this is the cause of most of the confusion over whether spirits are physical on nonphysical. Some observers may report a meeting with a spiritual being who seemed a normal man or woman of flesh and blood. The leader of the Hermetic Order of the Golden Dawn, Samuel L. MacGregor Mathers, wrote that he had met with the Secret Chiefs of the Order and that they appeared to be of flesh and blood.[1] Other observers may report that the spirits they saw were ghostly, or had body parts missing, or floated above the floor, or vanished into thin air in a moment.

It seems to me that the only way to reconcile these conflicting accounts is to assume that spirits are never physical, but appear physical. It explains why no credible spirit photograph has ever been taken. To the photographer viewing a spirit, it appears that he has a legitimate subject before his lens. Yet when the photo is developed, it contains nothing. The image of the spirit is a sensory metaphor in the mind of the photographer, and so cannot be conveyed to the recording medium. Yes, there are many strange and interesting photographs claimed to be photos of actual ghosts or angels, but I have studied them closely and find that either they are obvious fakes, or they are so vague that they could be virtually anything. I have never seen a conclusive spirit photograph, nor is such a photograph recognized by science. In my view, a true photograph of a spiritual being, imprinted in the usual manner upon the camera film or memory chip by light passing through a lens, is impossible.

SPIRITS PERCEIVE THE PHYSICAL WORLD
THROUGH THE SENSES OF PHYSICAL BEINGS

Just as the human mind cannot deal with the direct reality of spirits, neither can the spirit mind deal with the direct reality of our material universe. Spirits have no eyes to see, no ears to hear, no skin with which to feel, no nose to smell, and no tongue to taste. Without the intervention of a living body equipped with sense organs, the unique impression of reality that we receive through our senses would be denied to spirits. Yet spirits need to be able to perceive our reality in order to communicate in an intelligible way with us. They attain this perception by gathering sense impressions flowing through our physical senses and translating them into their own terms.

The practical consequence is that spirits can only see the world as we see it by gazing out at it through our human eyes. They are usually not accustomed to perceiving reality in this limited and physical way, so it is little wonder that they often make mistakes. Our perception of time must be a function of our physical sense processes. I can guess this because spirits have great difficulty handling time. They often give wildly incorrect dates or faulty estimates of the duration of events. They handle time so badly that no date predicted by a spirit is to be trusted. Their main error seems to be to compress time, so that what to a spirit appears to be a day may take a year in human terms.

We are most familiar with spirits that gaze out at our world through human eyes, because these are the spirits that communicate with us, but it may be that spirits exist who view the world through the senses of animals. We cannot know what the world would look like when seen through the eyes of a cat, or an eagle, only that it would seem slightly different than it does to us. If spirits can move from mind to mind, they may be able to dance from one creature to another, peeking out at our reality each time, and so may gain a multiple impression of the physical universe impossible for us to achieve, or even imagine. However, all these forms of perception of the material world require material senses—this is the important point. Without physical eyes to borrow the use of, spirits are blind. Without physical ears, they are deaf. Spirits need living creatures to experience the universe as we do.

SPIRITS ARE INTERESTED IN HUMANITY

Why would spirits wish to experience the physical universe? Different spirits will give different answers to this question. It is an essential perception of reality if they wish to communicate with human consciousness, but this raises an even more fascinating question: Why do spirits wish to communicate with us? I have considered this matter at great length. Of one thing I am convinced—humanity is important to spiritual beings. Most spirit communications arise spontaneously, as far as the person who perceives the spirit is concerned. Spirits initiate contact with human awareness.

They are perfectly able to remain hidden within the depths of the unconscious mind, peeking out at the material world through our physical senses, but they deliberately draw attention to themselves so that humans notice their existence. They have been doing this for thousands of years.

It may be that only a tiny percentage of spirits go to the effort to attract human attention. I have speculated that the unconscious is filled with countless spirits that have not the slightest interest in human affairs. They go about their business, ignoring human consciousness or oblivious to it. We would remain forever ignorant of not only the natures of these spirits but also of their very existence. They would be like the creatures dwelling deep in the ocean that never rise to the surface. To a person standing on the shore, only the smaller sea dwellers on the rocks, or those that thrust their heads above the water, would be visible. The leviathans of the deep would remain undisturbed, unperceived, unsuspected. Who knows what vast power these deep dwellers of the mind might possess, should they ever choose to rise to the surface of our awareness?

SPIRITS DERIVE SOME BENEFIT FROM HUMAN ASSOCIATION

We can only consider the spirits that have decided to make their existence known to us. The others, if indeed there are others, will remain forever hidden and unknown in the deeps of the mind. About those that show themselves to human awareness, it may be said that they evidently derive some benefit by interacting with us. The act of causing us to be aware of them, and interacting with them, itself gives them something they wish to acquire, or need. After years of considering the matter, I have concluded that spirits need emotions.

Spirits feed on emotions. By revealing themselves to us, by provoking reactions in us, they generate emotions of the type they seek. These revelations do not usually take place while we are awake. It is the more common practice for spirits to provoke our emotions while we sleep, by entering into our dreams and manipulating them. Different types of spirits appear to seek different emotions. Some seek to provoke refined, spiritual thoughts; others the most gross emotions of lust or terror. Nightmares are the result of spirits of the latter sort generating strong emotions upon which to feed.

It is possible to distinguish a self-aware spirit from a nonconscious dream character by observing its behavior. A spirit manipulating a dream will provoke abrupt changes in the flow of the dream story. When it becomes aware of your attention, it will step out of the dream drama, so to speak, and will regard you directly, often with an expression of malevolence or contempt. Spirits of a low type often transform ordinary dreams into sex dreams, so that they can feast on the stronger emotions, and even, I suspect, on the sensations of arousal and desire. These sensations of lust are a kind of thickened or materialized emotion.

When I write that spirits feed on emotions, I do not necessarily mean that they would waste away without emotional nourishment. Rather, emotions provide some sort of desirable energy to spirits, something that they can use for their own purposes. Higher spirits such as angels express higher purposes for interacting with human beings, but I suspect that at root, the reason why all spirits seek out human awareness is the same—to generate emotions. Angels merely feed on spiritual emotions of a higher type. Their motives are not fundamentally different from those of demons, who seek to provoke lustful or other powerful types of emotion. However, the behavior of angels in interaction with human beings is honorable and helpful, regardless of their primary motivation. A humble man will slap together a peanut butter sandwich when he is hungry; a sophisticated man may make a French soufflé; but the underlying motive is the same in both cases—hunger.

SPIRITS CAN CONTROL OR MODIFY HUMAN PERCEPTIONS

One consequence of sensory metaphors is that spirits potentially possess the ability to control human perceptions. Consider this statement. Spirits can control human perceptions. They can manipulate everything we see, hear, feel, smell, or taste. They can make anything they wish appear in the world in front of us, and by the same token they can make anything that is physically before us disappear. This is an awesome and terrifying power with incredible implications. A man whose senses are controlled by a spirit can never, at any time, be certain of what he sees or hears. The spirit can, if it wishes, cause him to see or hear anything, with absolute reality. So real are these illusions, when they are complete and function on all five sense channels, that it is utterly impossible to distinguish them from ordinary perceptions.

This may account for the fantastic eyewitness testimony that occurs so frequently throughout the history of spirit visitation. Witnesses to apparitions of various spirits, such as those who mask themselves and pretend to be Jesus or the

Virgin Mary, come forth with the most impossible state-
ments, and assert as fact matters that simply cannot be; yet
they are utterly convinced of what they have witnessed. For
example, the prophet Isaiah is supposed to have turned the
sun back in its course, an obvious impossibility (2 Kings
20:11). It was so real to those who saw it that it could not
be denied. The various other miracles reported in the Bible
can perhaps be explained in the same manner, as sensory
manipulations by spirits for their own purposes. For example, it may be that Moses did not transform his staff into a
serpent before Pharaoh, yet it appeared to become a serpent
to witnesses of the event because a spirit, or spirits, induced
an illusion into the minds of the watchers.

Spirits obviously have this control over human senses.
Without it, they could not appear before us. Usually it is
imperfect. Not all spirits can control all our perception of
sense impressions whenever they wish. When this control is
possessed by a spirit to perfection, however, that spirit can
cause the human being under its influence to seem to perceive anything. How often this takes place is impossible to
know, but I suspect it occurs much more frequently than
anyone imagines.

I suspect that there is a limit to this control. When Jesus
appeared to transform water into wine (John 2:5–10), he
was employing an illusion to deceive the senses. Perhaps if
the crowd had been twice as large, or ten times as large, it
would not have worked. Some might have seen the water as
wine, while others might have continued to see it as water.
However, in manipulating the impressions of a crowd using
sensory metaphors, it is not necessary to introduce illusions
into the minds of everyone, just a certain critical mass that

causes the rest present to doubt the evidence of their own senses. At a guess, this critical mass is probably around 10 percent. In any crowded place, if one out of ten persons declares loudly that there is an angel in the clouds, chances are that before too long there will be a general consensus that something out of the ordinary is in the clouds, even if many of the bewildered onlookers do not know precisely what it is.

Spirits can control human speech and actions

Just as there is no question that certain spirits can control human perceptions, so is there no doubt that some can manipulate human speech and actions. This is known as *possession*. It is far more common than most believe, because most possessions occur quietly, with the spirit that has assumed control of a human host taking great care not to draw attention to itself. It is only the most foolish and malicious of spirits who take control of a human host for the purpose of inflicting injury upon the host or other persons.

A friend of mine recently had her consciousness displaced by an angel. The angel sat watching television, then took her two children shopping. This is the usual kind of possession, but it is never written up in the tabloids because it does not involve projectile vomit or rotating heads. The children sensed that something was out of the ordinary only because their mother was uncharacteristically nice to them. Her personality changed, becoming more subdued. Later, the woman was able to confirm that she had been possessed by talking with the spirit, which was a familiar spirit with whom she had interacted for many months.

It can be difficult sometimes to distinguish between possession and schizophrenia. I am not certain that an absolute dividing line can be drawn between the two. The main difference is that the mind of the possessed person remains in complete control apart from the incident of the possession, whereas in schizophrenia, the mind that is displaced by an alternate personality is disordered and unable to distinguish reality from illusion. I have speculated to myself that the alternate personalities of schizophrenics may, indeed, be spirits who have been drawn to the foreground of consciousness by the vulnerability and confusion of the schizophrenic.

Mediumship and channeling (which are the same phenomenon) involve possession, although it is not called by this name. Whenever the consciousness of a human being is displaced by the consciousness of a spirit, possession has occurred. It happens not only to psychics but to average men and women on the street, and it may last only for a few seconds or a few minutes—just long enough for the possessing spirit to accomplish its purpose. It is my conviction that some of the more senseless murders that shock the public are committed by those who are momentarily possessed by malicious spirits who have waited for their chance to generate the most intense and densest possible human emotion, black despair.

It may be that some persons are by their natures more susceptible to possession than others, just as some individuals are more easily hypnotized than others. The average person seems to suffer little risk of possession by spirits while in an ordinary state of waking consciousness, but a significant minority of the population is naturally mediumistic. And just as we are easier to hypnotize when we want to be hypnotized, it may be that spirit possession happens most often to those who invite it upon themselves.

For example, possession sometimes occurs to those who experiment with the Ouija board for amusement, and who use the board to summon spirits to them. They open their minds to these spirits without being fully aware that they are doing it, and if they are mediumistic by nature, possession may occur. The possession in these instances is usually brief and harmless, akin to the possession that befalls charismatic Christians during church services.

SPIRITS ARE INTELLIGENT BEINGS

If a spirit can possess and control a human body, it is natural to speculate that spirits may not be too different, in their essential nature, from whatever lies at the base of human identity. In my opinion, human beings are only spirits who have been lucky enough, or unlucky enough, depending on how you look at it, to obtain vessels of flesh to inhabit. It is the residence within a body of flesh that over a period of years differentiates the human soul, in a superficial way, from the spirits who have no bodies of their own. When a spirit interacts with human beings regularly and often over an extended period, it becomes more and more human in its personality. This is due to the humanizing influence of our physical shell, specifically to the influence sensory input has on spirit personality. After viewing the material universe through human senses for enough years, a spirit in effect becomes human in its behavior.

Spirits can be highly intelligent. This is not always obvious because they often have difficulty expressing themselves in ordinary language, and because the different reality they usually inhabit causes them to think in a way that is unnatural for human beings. I have mentioned the difficulty spirits have with time. They have just as much trouble distinguishing truth from fiction. What spirits say is not to be trusted too readily. Most spirits do not lie deliberately; they just cannot always understand the difference between a lie and the truth, from the human perspective.

The more frequently a spirit possesses a human being, and interacts with other human beings, the easier it is for that spirit to estimate time intervals accurately, and to distinguish truth from fiction. It should not be wondered that spirits have difficulty with truth, when we consider that young children who have not been in the body too many years have exactly the same difficulty. Truth, or rather fact, must be a very fleshy concept.

Spirits often impersonate dead people, pretending to be the souls of once-living human beings who have returned to communicate with their relatives, or to convey to humanity important information. We can be fairly sure they are not the souls they pretend to be because, when asked for specific information confirming their human identities, such spirits are unable to provide it in a consistent way that precludes deception. Even so, such spirits actually believe themselves to be the people they impersonate.

Why do spirits impersonate the dead? It is my view that they are so eager for form and identity of their own that they seize upon any strong identity that is made available to them. In their essence spirits have no forms, no identities of their own. They assume forms when perceived through sensory metaphors. We give them names and personalities when we interact with them. The gods of pagan times are spirits who were given identities by their worshippers. The same process can occur when a single human being interacts with a spirit—the human mind supplies that spirit with a form that is akin to a suit of clothing for the spirit, which when naked would be invisible.

Just as we need spirits to take on an identity before we can interact with them, so also do spirits require identities —a sense of self—when using human senses to look out upon our material world, in order to process that information. Without form, without a sense of self, without a name, a spirit is unable to understand our reality in the way we understand it, and unless it understands our reality as we do, it cannot communicate with us or interact with us in meaningful ways. The spirit's understanding of our reality is never complete—hence the difficulty spirits have with the concepts of time and truth—but the longer a spirit interacts with humans, the more complete its understanding of our world becomes.

Those who consult mediums or channelers often seek communications from dead relatives or loved ones, or even from famous individuals who have died. Their emotions and expectations are strong. Spirits who are hungry for strong emotions, and who need identities in order to communicate and interact effectively with human beings, take the identities of the dead for their own, and they do so with such conviction that they often believe completely that they are the soul of the dead that they impersonate. They are not trying to deceive. They enter so completely into the identity of the dead person that they actually become the soul of that person, at least to their own conviction.

As to whether the souls of the dead ever do return to communicate with the living, it is my own belief that they do not. It is possible that in dying they leave an impression of themselves on certain localities—impressions that are picked up by sensitive individuals and are classed as ghosts—but as to the actual soul, the essence of the dead person, I do not think it ever returns. In taking this view, I realize that I am taking a minority position among occultists and psychics.

WHAT ARE THEY?

These are some of the observations about the nature of spirits that I have made over the past few decades of inter-action with them. The most important question remains unasked: What are they?

Different spirits offer different explanations for their own existence. Until the time of the European Renaissance, most spirits that communicated with human beings identified themselves as gods, or as angels, or as spirits of the natural world or of the heavens. A shift took place during the Spiri-tualism craze of the 19th century, and spirits began to over-whelmingly identify themselves as the souls of dead human beings. Perhaps this happened because it was easier for human beings, following the Industrial Revolution, to believe in the souls of the dead than in fairies, nymphs, and angels. More recently spirits have begun to identify themselves as aliens who dwell on other planets or in other dimensions of space. This tendency has paralleled the UFO phenomenon of the latter half of the 20th century.

I suspect that spirits no more understand why they exist than we do. They simply exist, a part of the grand scheme of creation that extends so much further than the boundaries of time and space. They are not material, but they are as real as we are. Indeed, we ourselves are spirits who possess vessels of flesh.

NOTES

1. Howe, p. 129.

4

Serpent of Wisdom

Why is the lowly snake so maligned? It is not obvious why such a harmless and useful creature should have received such bad press over the centuries. Snakes do far more good in the world than harm. They eat rodents, and without them, rats and mice would be a much more serious plague than they usually are. The Maoists in China found this out once, when they tried to eradicate snakes and ended up with an exploding rat population. Both rats and mice breed prolifically in the absence of natural predators that keep their numbers in check. When their numbers increase, they eat the grain in the fields and in the storehouses, resulting in famines. This has been a problem for the peoples of the world since the dawn of history.

There are many venomous species of snakes, it is true, but the majority of snakes are not deadly, and even vipers will not strike at a human being unless provoked. So why the eternal, unreasoned hatred? Many Christians will kill every snake they see, regardless of its species or what it is doing. The snake is proverbial in folklore for a liar, a deceiver, a doer of evil—a reputation that has no connection with its benign and useful existence in nature.

SERPENT IN THE GARDEN

The assassination of the snake's character started way back with the biblical myth of the Garden of Eden and the Fall of Man. This myth is older than the Hebrews who preserved it in the first book of their Torah. It originated in Mesopotamia. Unfortunately, those parts of the Babylonian myth that preserve the account of the Serpent tempting Eve have not survived, as George Smith mentioned in his work *The Chaldean Account of Genesis*:

> The loss of this portion of the Creation legend is unfortunate, as, however probable it may be that the Hebrew and Babylonian traditions agree about the Garden and the Tree of Knowledge, we cannot now prove it.[1]

In the Babylonian myth, the part of the Serpent was played by the dragon of the sea, a creature of Tiamat that bears a name meaning "the scaly one." A Babylonian seal preserved at the British Museum shows a man and a woman seated facing each other, with a tree between them. The tree has seven branches. We can assume that one figure is male and the other female because one wears horns and the other does not. I think the horned figure is the male, but of course there's no way to prove it. The two figures reach out their hands to take fruit from the tree. Behind what I take to be the woman undulates a snake, its head near to the ear of the woman.[2] It is probable that this seal depicts the eating of the fruit from the Tree of Knowledge. The snake is probably intended to be the dragon of the sea.

> The dragon which, in the Chaldean account of the Creation, leads man to sin, is the creature of Tiamat, the living principle of the sea and of chaos, and he is an embodiment of the spirit of chaos or disorder which was opposed to the deities at the creation of the world.
>
> It is clear that the dragon is included in the curse for the Fall, and that the gods invoke on the head of the human race all the evils which afflict humanity.[3]

In the Hebrew account that has come down to us as part of the book of Genesis, the Serpent is not identified, but the usual presumption of Jews and Christians is that it is the Adversary in disguise. The Adversary is the angel who rebelled against and opposes the will of God, and who goes under various names, such as Samael, Satan, and Lucifer.

In the Hebrew myth, God tells Adam and his mate that they may eat from any tree in the Garden of Eden, but must not eat of the fruit of the tree that is in the midst of the Garden, or they will surely die. The snake offers another opinion:

> And the serpent said unto the woman, Ye shall not surely die:

For God doth know that in the day ye eat thereof, then your eyes shall be opened, and ye shall be as gods, knowing good and evil.

And when the woman saw that the tree was good for food, and that it was pleasant to the eyes, and a tree to be desired to make one wise, she took of the fruit thereof, and did eat, and gave also unto her husband with her; and he did eat.[4]

THE GNOSTIC SERPENT

This brief account is fascinating for a number of reasons. One puzzle is the motivation of the Serpent. The usual Christian explanation is that the Serpent was trying to hurt mankind, by seducing the woman to violate the command of God. However, the Gnostics had another explanation, which was that the Serpent was an agent sent from a higher deity to reveal to mankind our true divine nature, which the god of the Garden had concealed.

In the Gnostic text titled the *Apocryphon of John*, the Serpent in the Garden is Christ before his embodiment, who is transformed into an eagle that descends to perch on the top of the Tree of Knowledge. The Serpent itself is not redeemed in this document, but rather, displaced, and still relegated to the role of evil-doer, the obedient servant of the angry god of the Garden, Yaldabaoth—the name given by the Ophites and Sethians to the Demiurge or craftsman who fashioned the material universe.

And I said to the savior, "Lord was it not the serpent who taught Adam to eat?" The savior smiled and said, "The serpent taught them to eat from wickedness, begetting lust and destruction, that he might be useful to him."[5]

That is, useful to Yaldabaoth, in keeping Adam and Eve distracted by passions, so that they should remain in ignorance.

Christ goes on to say:

> I appeared in the form of an eagle on the tree of knowledge, which is the Epinoia from the foreknowledge of the pure light, that I might teach them and awaken them out of the depth of sleep.[6]

Epinoia is a Greek concept meaning, in this context, creative awareness or enlightenment. The Epinoia was in Gnosticism one of the higher expressions of the divine. In this Gnostic text, the eagle is the Serpent symbolically transformed from a creature of chaos to a creature of light. In this way, the text of Genesis regarding the Serpent is not so much denied, but reinterpreted. Instead of the Serpent acting in defiance of the god of the Garden, he acts as a servant of that god. The role he is usually believed to have fulfilled, the opening of the eyes of Eve, is given to Christ.

This transformation does not occur in all Gnostic texts. In most of them, it is indeed the Serpent who opens the eyes of Adam and Eve to their innate divinity, and causes them to realize that they are superior to the god they formerly worshipped. Irenaeus, a bishop of the Christian church in Gaul during the second century, wrote about what the Gnostics believed concerning the Serpent:

But their mother (wisdom) cunningly led Eve and
Adam astray, by the agency of the snake, so that they
transgressed the commandment of Ialdabaoth. And
Eve was easily persuaded, as if she were listening to
an offspring of god. And she persuaded Adam to eat
from the tree from which god had said not to eat.
Moreover—they say—when they ate they became
acquainted with that power which is superior to all,
and they revolted from those who had made them.[7]

The mother is the great womb of creation, Barbelo, who
for Gnostics is the first emanation from the highest divinity and the supreme Goddess, but here she takes her active
and more youthful projected form of Sophia (Wisdom).
According to Irenaeus, the Serpent serves the will of Sophia,
in transmitting *gnosis* (spiritual enlightenment) to humanity.

THE OPHITES

The Ophites, an early Gnostic sect that flourished in the
first century, were direct about their admiration for the Serpent, and celebrated it as the liberator of humanity from
our sleep of ignorance. For this reason they were despised
by the fathers of the Christian Church as serpent worshipers. But the Serpent in the Garden was only the agent of a
higher power, and it is this power, the divine Wisdom in the
form of Sophia, or in later sects, the heavenly Christ, which
they revered, not the Serpent itself.

The fourth-century father of the Christian Church,
Epiphanius of Salamis, wrote in his work *Panarion* that
the Ophites (who are number 37 in his list of 80 heresies)
employed a serpent in their communion service, a practice

he regarded as an abomination. The snake was kept in a chest that bore the name *cista mystica*. At the beginning of the service the snake was released and allowed to undulate over the rolls of bread that would serve as the communion feast. The bread was then broken and eaten by the Ophite worshipers, who each kissed the snake on the mouth.

> "The Ophites," he observes, "attribute all wisdom to the serpent of paradise, and say that he was the author of knowledge to men." "They keep a live serpent in a chest; and at the time of the mysteries entice him out by placing bread before him upon a table. Opening his door he comes out, and having ascended the table, folds himself about the bread. This they call a perfect sacrifice. They not only break and distribute this among the votaries, but whosoever will, may kiss the serpent. This the wretched people call the Eucharist. They conclude the mysteries by singing an hymn through him to the supreme Father.[8]

Epiphanius regarded this as worship of the serpent, but it was more a matter of worship through the serpent, in the same way Catholics worship through images of the saints. It is significant that he wrote that the Ophites sang a hymn "through" the serpent, not "to" the serpent.

PENTECOSTAL SNAKE-HANDLING

The parallels between this Orphic practice described by Epiphanius, and the modern Christian practice of dancing with serpents that is used by charismatic churches in America, is too obvious to require emphasis.

Snake-handling among the Pentecostals is said to have begun one day in 1910 when preacher George Went Hensley took a box containing a rattlesnake to the pulpit during a church service, lifted out the snake with his bare hands to show his faith in the literal word of Mark 16:18 ("they shall take up serpents"), and then challenged the assembled congregation to touch and hold the serpent.

The Pentecostals cannot be said to worship the snakes they handle, any more than the Ophites worshipped the snake they allowed to coil upon the communion bread. Still, in both cases a strange degree of respect and importance is given to the serpent, transforming it into a sacred creature, in the case of the Ophites to be honored, and in the case of the Pentecostals to be mastered. In both instances the snake becomes an agent of the divine, an object of faith.

Those with a knowledge of Kabbalah may find it interesting that the Hebrew word for serpent (*nachash*) has a numerical value of 358, which is the same numerical value as the Hebrew word for the Messiah (*mashiach*).[9] The significance of this correspondence from a Gnostic point of view cannot be overstated.

SERPENT WORSHIP AMONG THE PAGANS

Although the Gnostics did not worship the serpent directly, serpent worship was common throughout the pagan world. Serpent mounds are found in America, such as the famed Serpent Mound in Adams County, Ohio. The monumental Stone Age earthen construction at Avebury, in England, is serpentine. Serpents, in the forms of dragons or sea serpents, adorn Saxon and Celtic jewelry, weapons, and manuscripts—indeed, the folklore that Saint Patrick drove all the serpents from Ireland, which had no indigenous serpents to drive out, may have arisen from a battle of theologies between early Christians and pagan serpent worshipers. The cult of the serpent stayed strong in Scandinavia for centuries after Christianity had achieved control over the rest of Europe, and is found throughout the art of the Vikings, whose very ships bore dragon heads and were called dragons of the sea. In Norse mythology, the Midguard serpent was supposed to encircle the entire world. In is a common belief in many diverse cultures, both ancient and modern.

The serpent was not always reviled. The Greeks regarded the snake as the wisest of creatures, and immortal. This latter bit of folklore probably arose from the way a snake appears to renew its youth and vitality every time it sheds its skin. The new skin beneath the old is smooth and shining. Perhaps because of its reputation for deathlessness, the serpent was the symbol of the god of healing, Asclepius. It twines around his staff, which is the origin for the modern symbol for the medical profession.

We see it also in the staff of Hermes, swift messenger of the gods who was renowned for his wisdom. The staff of Asclepius has a single serpent entwined around it, whereas the staff of Hermes, called a caduceus, has two serpents coiled on its shaft. Both staffs are used by various medical organizations as their symbol, although the staff of Asclepius is the more correct symbol for healers.

These two admirable qualities—wisdom and power over death—characterized the beliefs held by the pagans of the

classical world toward snakes. How different from the superstitious impulse among less enlightened Christians that all
snakes must be killed on sight.

Notes

1. Smith, p. 88.

2. Ibid., p. 91.

3. Ibid.

4. Genesis 3:4–6.

5. Robinson, p. 111.

6. Ibid.

7. Layton, p. 175.

8. Bathurst, pp. 88–89.

9. Godwin, p. 270.

5

Familiars

The history of familiars extends as far back as that of magic itself. The word immediately evokes an image of a witch's black cat. Familiars are generally thought to be pet animals that possess magic power and preternatural intelligence. They are supposed to come and go in a twinkling to carry out the secret purposes of the witch. As is true for most clichés, this conception is not completely incorrect, but it is limited and misleading. Familiars are not animals, but spirits. Witches may have familiars, but so do many others who practice different kinds of magic, and even those with no interest in the esoteric.

A familiar is any spirit that maintains a personal relationship with a human being. It is the close contact and communication between human and spirit that makes a familiar relationship, not the type of spirit or the magical practices of the person. Communication is a key factor. A spirit who intervenes in the life of a human being cannot be classed as a familiar if the person lacks conscious awareness of the spirit. Everyone is said to have his or her own guardian angel, but a guardian angel usually does not qualify as a familiar simply because, in most cases, it does not communicate with the person under its care. Were a guardian angel to begin appearing on a regular basis and interacting with an individual, it would then be a familiar. This sometimes occurs in ceremonial magic and is known as the conversation of the holy guardian angel.[1]

THE HOLY GUARDIAN ANGEL

Obtaining the conversation of the holy guardian angel is the central ritual purpose of the European grimoire known in English as *The Book of the Sacred Magic of Abramelin the Mage*, which was translated from an incomplete French manuscript and published by the British magician S. L. MacGregor Mathers in 1898. This grimoire also contains sets of letter squares designed to act as magic talismans, but they are not fully presented in the French text that Mathers had at his disposal.

The grimoire is actually German in origin and is believed to have been written by the 14th-century Jew Rabbi Jacob ben Moses ha Levi Moellin. In 1995 a German-language version of the text edited by Georg Dehn was published based on German manuscripts and a German edition first issued in 1725. This contains the completed squares. It has since been translated into English (Ibis Publishing, 2006). However, the French version published by Mathers gives the ritual for contacting the holy guardian angel in a useable form and has been a mainstay of Western occultism for more than a century.

Mathers was the most active of the three earthly chiefs of the Hermetic Order of the Golden Dawn, an English occult society that established its first temple in 1888 in London. As a result of his study of *Abramelin*, the process of obtaining the conversation of the holy guardian angel became the highest magical goal for members of that order, including among them such literary figures as Aleister Crowley and A. E. Waite. Crowley was especially obsessed with the ritual of the holy guardian angel. He went so far as to buy a house in Scotland in 1899 where he could work the ritual in comparative seclusion. It was this spirit, which called itself Aiwass, that in 1904 transmitted to Crowley his *Liber AL vel Legis*, better known as the *Book of the Law*, in which the doctrine of Thelema, Crowley's occult philosophy, is laid forth.

In Mathers' version of the *Abramelin* grimoire, contacting the holy guardian angel requires six months of intense preparation—in the German version of the work it is eighteen months. The key to success is purification of the mind and body. Through cleansing the magician, it focused on the single purpose of establishing communication with his guardian angel. The ritual work consists mainly of repeated daily prayers and meditation. A very unusual aspect of the ritual process in the grimoire is the disregard of astrological times such as the days of the week and the magic hours of the day. The author of the grimoire considered the observance of times to be vain when dealing with so exalted a spiritual matter.

The holy guardian angel is considered to be the highest spiritual intelligence with which it is possible for a human being to interact on a personal level—the ultimate familiar. Lesser familiars can be contacted using much less elaborate ritual workings.

Indeed, familiar spirits are eager to form a bond with serious magicians. All that is usually necessary is to open your mind to their presence by ritually invoking them on a daily basis. Crowley asserted that the most important thing in seeking the conversation of the holy guardian angel was to invoke often—the same is good advice even if you are trying to obtain communication with a lesser familiar.

DISPELLING MISCONCEPTIONS ABOUT FAMILIARS

Several common misconceptions about familiars must be dismissed before we examine their general nature. They are often understood to be the slaves or servants of the witch or magician to whom they are attached. They are thought to be bound against their will to their master by the force of magic, and constrained to obey by threats of punishment. They are considered to be evil spirits either summoned to the service of a witch or magician by black magic, or appointed by the Devil to serve those who make a black pact.

It is true that some magicians summon and bind lesser spirits to act as their servants. However, familiars are not always lesser spirits, nor are they always constrained against their will. More often, the bond between a human and a familiar is one of friendship and mutual respect. There is no need to bind or threaten the spirit, who acts in cooperation with the magician as a partner to aid his or her purposes. The feelings between human and familiar are usually affectionate, even loving. Spirits constrained to serve by threats of punishment make very poor familiars who cannot be trusted, but those who help willingly from a motive of friendship or love need no constraint.

Familiars are often spirits of a high order, capable of full communication with human beings. They may even possess an intelligence superior to that of their human partner and act as a guide and teacher, especially in spiritual and esoteric matters. In traditional Western occultism of the Renaissance, establishing a relationship with a familiar was the first step in learning magic. The familiar conveyed the practical ritual procedures needed by the magician, and enabled the magician to make first contact with other spirits and to learn their names and sigils. Indeed, the view is expressed in some of the grimoires that the method for forming a link with a familiar is all that is required, since the familiar will then provide any additional information the magician needs.

This process is very clearly expressed in the communications of the Elizabethan magician Dr. John Dee with the Enochian angels. Dee became aware that spirits were seeking to communicate with him when they made repeated rapping noises in his bedchamber at night. He hired a succession of crystal gazers to enable the spirits to speak to him. Through these mediums the spirits gave Dee instructions as to what ritual furniture he was to build and what sigils he was to make in order to better communicate with them. His initial communications with them involved nothing more than prayer and invocation, but they soon delivered to him the complex structure of what we know today as Enochian magic, a complete system of rituals and invocations unlike any that had existed in the world up until that time.

One of the Enochian spirits came into the crystal in the form of a little girl who identified herself as Madimi. She served as Dee's personal familiar, and acted as an intermediary between Dee and other higher teaching angels with information to give to Dee. Dee thought so well of this little familiar that he named one of his own daughters Madimia, after the spirit. He always greeted her with love and respect.

Familiars are seldom evil spirits held against their will. This would make little sense, since such spirits would forever try to escape or betray the magician, and would require constant watching. They would be far more trouble than they are worth. The notion that familiars are evil arose from the anti-magic propaganda of the Church during the witch craze of the 16th and 17th centuries. Priests viewed all relationships between humans and spirits as inherently evil and consequently as devilish, since all evil was supposed to arise from the actions of the Devil.

Women accused of witchcraft were coerced into confessing many untruths, among them that they kept as their servants familiar spirits who helped them commit acts of evil; that they suckled and fed these creatures on their own blood; that the familiars took the forms of pet animals with monstrous or fantastic features, and could appear or disappear at will; that their familiars or imps were assigned to them as servants by Satan himself, after the witch signed a pact pledging her life to works of evil in return for magic power.

These malicious lies were told and published so often that many otherwise sensible people believed them. They are still believed by members of the Christian fundamentalist movement, who regard the execution of thousands of innocent women for witchcraft as a good thing, and view a devil with horns and a pitchfork as a real and ever-present threat.

The truth is less black and white. As there are good and evil human beings, so are there good and evil familiars.

Care must be exercised when choosing a familiar spirit, just as we must exercise caution before entering into a sustained partnership with another person. Spirits are capable of deception, but also of honesty. Some are malicious, others loving and kind. They have their own complex personalities, and may be cheerful one day but moody the next. They exhibit great nobility, but also spite and pettiness. What is true of spirits in general is also true of familiars, because familiars form a broad cross section of the spirit population. Almost any type of spirit may become a familiar.

Familiars in shamanism, witchcraft, ceremonial magic, and spiritualism

There are four areas of the Western esoteric tradition where familiars play a prominent role: shamanism, witchcraft, ceremonial magic, and spiritualism. It is worth considering each briefly when seeking to understand familiars.

In traditional shamanism, familiar spirits were vital to the magic of the shaman or shamaness. A young shaman was chosen as a partner by a spirit, who remained with him throughout his life. It became the shaman's celestial or heavenly wife—or in the case of a shamaness, celestial husband. Often the shaman had no say in the matter. He was chosen by the spirit. Or the shaman and spirit agreed mutually on the union. This spirit bride of the shaman was the most important single component in the success or failure of his career. The more powerful the spirit bride, the more powerful the shaman. The relationship was sexual. A shaman was not prevented from having a mortal wife, but the spirit wife was always first in his affections. In addition to this primary familiar, shamans used a number of lesser spirits as servants to fulfill specific functions. These would also be classed as familiars, although they were subordinate in importance and power to the spirit wife of the shaman, who was the equal, if not the superior, of the shaman.

Shamans interacted with other spirits on a regular basis, chief among them the totemic spirits of animal species such as the bear or the wolf, with whom the shaman believed himself to share a common ancestry. The bond between the shaman and these animal spirits was not as close as the bond between the shaman and his spirit wife, but it might rise to the level of a familiar relationship. The shaman regarded the animal spirits as members of his own clan and shared mutual obligations with them. He was required to help and respect the species related to him, and in return expected some consideration from these beasts who were his distant relatives. The animal spirit interacting with the shaman was a kind of ruling spirit of the species, and expressed its collective intelligence and life force.

Ancient witchcraft arose out of shamanism, so it is not surprising that it would share shamanic characteristics. The familiar spirits of witchcraft are the descendants of the heavenly wife and spirit servants of shamanism. It may be that we associate familiar spirits in witchcraft with animals because of the strong link between the shaman and his animal totems. The familiar pet of the medieval witch is a kind of shamanic animal spirit guide, much reduced in stature.

There are practical reasons why a familiar spirit would choose to inhabit the body of a pet animal. Possession of the animal allows the spirit to use the animal's senses to perceive the physical world—spirits can only perceive the material world as we perceive it through the senses of living creatures, either animal or human. Also, by inhabiting the body of a pet, the familiar is able to remain in close contact with the witch, and to receive the affection and attention of the witch without attracting unwanted notice.

During the witch craze, there was confusion as to the exact nature of the animal familiars of witches. The general consensus of the priests was that a familiar was a demonic creature that had assumed a material form resembling a pet animal in order to remain near to the witch while concealing its identity from others. It was thought that familiars were corporeal, yet possessed the power of changing their shapes at will, or disappearing in an instant. The truth is somewhat more complicated. Familiar spirits did at times possess the bodies of pet animals in order to draw upon their vitality and to use their senses to perceive the physical world. They could enter or leave these animals at will, and did not always remain within them. They also sometimes appeared in the images of beasts but without solid bodies of flesh and blood, so that to an onlooker they might seem to be a dog or a cat, yet still be able to change shape in a moment or vanish, because they were not constrained by material forms. Familiars might also appear to a witch in human form or remain invisible while communicating with the witch.

The fable that witches fed their familiars on the blood of their bodies also has a grain of truth. Familiar spirits derive a form of vitality from the emotions of their human associates, particularly from strong emotions such as love. This is one reason why spirits are drawn to human beings, and form close unions with humans. Human emotion and human attention have the effect of fixing or solidifying the forms and identities of familiar spirits, so that over time the personality of a familiar becomes more stable, its self-awareness more consistent.

Familiars played a less important, yet still significant, role in traditional Western ceremonial magic, sometimes known as high magic. Ceremonial magic is all about control—the magician seeks to command the forces of nature, the actions of spirits, even the gods. Familiar spirits are more apt to fulfill a subservient role in high magic. This did not prevent them from becoming the close friends of magicians. As mentioned earlier in this chapter, John Dee lavished the same affection he gave to his own children on the familiar spirit named Madimi. The German magician Cornelius Agrippa, who lived a century or so before Dee's time, had two black dogs that went everywhere with him, and he loved these dogs so much, he even let them sleep in the same bed with him. It was believed by priests of the Catholic Church that the dogs were familiar spirits of Agrippa, and this is quite possible, although it seems more likely to me that Agrippa's personal familiar was kept by him inside a ring that he wore.

Over the past hundred and fifty years or so, familiars are most often observed within the records of spiritualism. The spirit guide of the traditional trance medium is a familiar. The role of the spirit guide is to act as an intermediary between the medium and the spirit world, and also to serve the medium as teacher and protector. Its function is similar to that of the heavenly bride of the ancient shaman, although the union between a trance medium and a spirit guide is not always sexual in nature. Just how often the relationship was sexual is difficult to determine—the subject would not have been openly discussed during the Victorian period, when spiritualism was at its peak of popularity.

The modern equivalent of the séance medium is the channeler. Channelers rely on fewer theatrical apparatuses than the mediums of the Victorian era, but they function in the same way. They have their own spirit contacts who serve them as familiars. Some of these familiars, such as Seth, the spirit who communicated for many years with Jane Roberts, have written their own books, using their human associates as their physical instruments. It can be difficult to determine who is in control in such relationships, channeler or familiar. At their best, they are partnerships between equals. Another such relationship is that which existed between Alice A. Bailey and a spirit she referred to as "the Tibetan." Although the Tibetan claimed to be a living man with a physical body,[2] it seems clear to me that he was a spirit.

Familiars have always played a central role in Western esotericism. Whether acting as teachers, guides, protectors, or servants, they help to bridge the gulf between the human world and the spirit world. It would not be an exaggeration to state that without a familiar relationship with a spirit, the highest attainment in the art of magic is impossible. What is truly esoteric is always conveyed directly to the magician through the familiar, and can be learned in no other way.

Notes

1. Mathers, *Abramelin*, pp. xxvi, 85.

2. Bailey, p. vii.

6

Vampires, Werewolves, Ghosts, and Demons

I come here to tell you that vampires, werewolves, ghosts, and demons are real. That's right, real. All of them. None of this "it's only in your imagination" bullshit that you get from clinical psychologists. They are real beings with their own identities, purposes, and abilities. They interact with us, sometimes in ways that threaten our health and security.

They have always walked among us, from the earliest beginnings of human history, and probably long before we started writing down our experiences. How do we know? Because history is filled with eyewitness accounts of them, going back for thousands of years. When we read numerous accounts of encounters with these supernatural creatures, from all around the globe, ranging over a span of many centuries, why should we assume anything other than that they do, indeed, exist?

The question is, what manner of existence do they have? It obviously isn't a simple physical existence, or they would long ago have been recognized by science and stalked, killed, stuffed, and mounted in museums. Like Bigfoot and UFO aliens, they exist in some elusive, incorporeal form that defies physical proof of their existence. They cannot be captured and imprisoned. They cannot even be recorded on photographic film or video, despite many claims to the contrary. Yet to those who interact with them, they can seem as real, as solid, as tangible, as a rock or a tree.

Herein arises the confusion. Those who encounter a spiritual being may feel its touch, may see it before them, may hear its voice, yet it is impossible to record the presence of the creature on any material recording medium. No wonder few others believe them. No wonder many who have had these encounters choose to remain silent rather than be viewed by their neighbors as insane.

Revealed here is the true nature of vampires, werewolves, ghosts, and demons. Read it if you are feeling brave, and dismiss it if you can. For if you choose to believe, you may never have another quiet night's sleep.

Vampires

Everyone thinks they know what vampires are, how they are made, what they do, how they are killed. Such conceit is inevitable given the constant stream of vampire movies and novels. We love vampires. At least, we love to read about them or watch them on a screen. We are not so enthusiastic about them when we actually encounter them face to face. What we sometimes forget in our vicarious enjoyment of them is that they are dangerous, and very frightening.

Forget about the guy from Transylvania in a red cape. He is not a vampire; he is a nut with a mental problem. True vampires are not corporeal beings at all; they are spirits. They do not suck blood, they imbibe life force. So why the folklore about blood drinking? Because blood has been recognized since biblical times as the seat of the life force in the human body, and in the ritual animal sacrifices of the ancient Hebrews was reserved for God. Hence the expression "Blood is the life," which derives from the Old Testament: "But flesh with the life thereof, which is the blood thereof, shall ye not eat."[1]

The vitality of living things is distributed throughout their bodies, but it is recognized by occult and religious lore to be concentrated in certain places—notably in the blood and the semen. Which is why menstrual blood and semen have always had potent though forbidden uses in ceremonial magic both in the West and in the East.

A vampiric spirit is a spirit that deliberately draws off vitality from a human being, feeding on that vitality and making itself stronger and more clearly manifest on the material plane, while its prey becomes progressively weaker and more listless. Eventually a person obsessed by such a vampiric spirit may commit suicide from sheer despair, or may contract a fatal illness due to the weakened state of the body.

This is the reality of vampires, from which the silly legend of a blood-sucking corpse arose. The source of the legend explains many of its features.

How can the vampire of movie fame turn to a mist and rise up through the grave earth, or pass under a door? Because a true vampire is not physical in the first place, and so is not hindered by physical barriers.

Why is the movie vampire unable to see his reflection, if he is a physical being? Well, he cannot be a physical being if he is a vampire, because vampires are not physical. They are spirits that project themselves into the human mind in the form of sensory metaphors and in this way create the perception of a physical body. A spirit casts no reflection, so naturally a vampire of this type standing in front of a mirror would not be reflected—unless that spirit made a deliberate effort to create the illusion of a reflection.

How can the movie vampire change shape so easily? Because the true vampire on which his myth is based has no fixed, solid shape, but can change its appearance at will, or even make itself invisible. This is so because the true vampire does not really exist on the physical plane, but on the astral plane. It is perceived to be present on the physical plane by those human beings who seem to see it, but this is merely an illusion.

Sometimes humans exhibit this same vampiric thirst for the life force of others. Usually they are not even conscious of what they are doing. They seek out certain susceptible individuals they can easily bend to their will, and then spend time in their company, slowing drawing off the vitality of their companions by psychic means, until they are robust and hearty, while their unfortunate companions are listless and weak. Should the victim die or lose his reason, the human vampire moves on to another similar friend and haunts his presence so that the feeding may continue.

What is going on in these cases of human vampirism? It is often referred to as *psychic vampirism*, because it does not involve the actual drinking of blood. My suspicion is that a vampiric spirit has taken up residence within the mind of the human being, transforming him or her into a human vampire. The person involved is usually unaware of the presence of this parasitic spirit, which does not feed directly on the vitality of its host, but on susceptible companions of the host.

At times human vampires become aware of what they are doing to others. They may even glory in their power. It is not their power at all, but the power of a spirit that is merely using them as its vehicle, the way a man rides a horse in order to get where he wants to go.

If you happen to be in the presence of another person who makes you feel depressed and drained of vitality, and if that person seems to seek you out with an almost feverish enthusiasm, look into the eyes of the person. Look beyond the surface, and you may catch a glimpse of the thing that is hidden within, watching you the way a cat watches a bird. It would be in your best interests to avoid this person's company, if you value your good health.

WEREWOLVES

Almost as popular as vampires in the movies and in novels are werewolves. The myths of shapeshifters who can assume the forms of various beasts are as old as human history. They go all the way back to the earliest records of shamanic magic. The shaman is always a shapeshifter, able to enter the spirit world and put on the bodies of certain beasts with which he has a natural affinity. This trait runs right across the spectrum of shamanism, both ancient and modern, both East and West. Often the animal of shamanic transformation is a bird, but it can be others, such as a leopard, or a bear, or a wolf.

It is difficult to say why wolves were fixed upon as the basis for the modern movie legend of the were-creature, over all other beasts. Perhaps it was because the wolf is a beast of romance, both frightening and fascinating at the same time. Or it may have been due to the prevalence of werewolf folklore in Europe, where many Hollywood film makers and screen writers had their births.

Are werewolves real? Of course they are. Why else would there be so many historical accounts and legends about them? Are they real in a physical sense, the way your cell phone is real? No, of course not. If they were, we would see werewolf heads mounted in hunting lodges. Like the true vampire, the true werewolf is spiritual in nature.

Human beings have the ability to project awareness onto the astral plane. The astral plane is plastic rather than fixed. This means that it can change its appearance, its forms, its climate, and even the shapes of its inhabitants very easily. Think of the astral plane as a kind of dream world, for that is what it is. Dreams are a type of astral travel. Projection of awareness into the astral world takes place either deliberately or unconsciously. Unconscious projection is much more common.

We all project ourselves onto the astral plane when we dream. Usually we project ourselves as our common physical forms, but sometimes we project in the forms of animals, or in bestial forms that are half-animal and half-human. In this way, we may become were-beasts in our sleep. There is some anecdotal evidence that this happens more often to those of a very vicious, bloodthirsty temperament, who have trouble controlling their emotions and their actions.

Usually those projecting in the astral can pass the astral shadows of other human beings without being observed—waking humans seldom see an astral form that passes near them. On rare occasions, they do see the astral projection of another person, and then they believe they have seen a ghost or a doppelganger, or that they have hallucinated. More commonly, they feel the presence of a projected astral being as a coolness when they are touched. That is to say, if you project yourself onto the astral plane, and encounter the astral reflection of your cousin, that person may feel a coolness if you try to touch his astral body with your astral hand.

To the person projecting on the lowermost astral level, it appears that they move through the physical world. On the lower astral level the physical world is visible and seems quite solid and real, except that the astral traveler can do miraculous things, such as walk through walls or fly through the air. Consider your dreams. While you are dreaming, you move through a world that seems to be the physical world, but sometimes your dream-form does curious things—levitating, for example. You do not actually move through the physical world when you dream, you move through an astral world that very closely resembles the physical world, and which may reflect parts of the physical world.

The consequence of all this is that a vicious, bloodthirsty man may, when he falls asleep, assume the shape of a wolf or a wolflike being on the astral level. If he retains self-awareness, he may seem to himself to move through the physical world. His projected form may be so substantial that it may even be visible to other human beings who are awake, when that astral shapeshifter crosses a part of the lower astral plane that is in close conjunction with a part of the physical plane. The astral and the physical at times overlap to waking consciousness, and astral forms may briefly be seen or felt as though they existed on the physical plane.

This is the myth of the werewolf. People do sometimes see astral projections of other human beings that have bestial or partially bestial forms. On rare occasions, they can feel the touch of these astral were-creatures just as clearly as though they possessed physical flesh.

Part of the myth of the werewolf is that the person who changes into a wolf does not remember what was done during the change. This is based on the difficulty most people have remembering their astral projections, and what events transpired while they were traveling across the astral plane.

There are a few magicians who are able to deliberately project themselves into the astral world and retain their awareness. They can change their astral body into the form of an animal. Shamans did this in order to assume the power of their totemic beast, so that they could draw upon its power in the astral world. But most werewolves and other were-beasts are projected unconsciously, and those who transform into these creatures on the astral plane have no memory of what they did there after they return to normal consciousness.

Another form of were-animal should be mentioned, since some readers of this essay will be aware of it. A magician is able to give form and vitality to a concept on the astral level, shaping and refining that idea until it becomes as real and as solid astrally as a rock is physically solid. In this way astral creatures can be created by the action of the mind. Spirits deliberately created are referred to as *telesmatic images* in the magical system of the Golden Dawn. At times a very strong magician may unconsciously create an astral creature without meaning to do so. When a group brings forth such an unconscious creation, it is known as an *egregore*. When an individual does so, the shamanic magicians of Tibet call it a *tulpa*.

A tulpa may be formed either deliberately or unconsciously, during sleep or during prolonged meditation. As a tulpa continues to function on the astral level, it becomes more self-aware and more independent. Sometimes these created astral beings become so real that others can see them in dreams, or even while awake. If a magician is wrestling with violent and bloodthirsty emotions, and unconsciously creates such a tulpa, it may have the form of a wild beast.

Werewolves can be created in this way by magicians, either deliberately or unconsciously. Such astral werewolves may seek out other human beings and prey upon their energies by triggering intense fear and dread. They may obsess or haunt a person whom they find especially susceptible to their presence, and may draw off vital energy from that person over a period of weeks or months. Tulpas can become so independent of the magician who gave them birth that they break free completely from the control of the magician and live their own astral existence.

Ghosts

The mythology of ghosts has evolved over the centuries in surprising ways, becoming less threatening with the passage of time. For the ancient Egyptians and Greeks, ghosts were to be feared for very practical reasons. They were thought capable of murdering the living and, by the Egyptians, of consuming the flesh of the living. There is considerable crossover between the early myth of the ghost and the myths of the vampire and the werewolf. A ghost was believed by the ancient Egyptians to return to its living family members to kill them and feast on their flesh.

Our own ghosts share one feature in common with the ancient shades of the dead—they are thought to be the spiritual remains of a once-living human being. A ghost is not an inhuman spiritual creature, but an aspect of a deceased person that has lingered on or near the earthly plane. At least, this is the belief. Ghosts do not actually inhabit the material plane, any more than any other spiritual creature inhabits the physical realm. They are inhabitants of the lower astral world who at times become perceptible to living human beings—often to their close family members or friends.

Ghosts can be surprisingly persistent, appearing to the living for spans of centuries. They usually haunt a specific physical locality, often the places where they died or were murdered—for it is believed that the dead most often become restless, wandering shades when their deaths are unnatural. Not everyone sees ghosts. Some psychic individuals are particularly prone to glimpses of these eerie echoes of the formerly living.

There are certain general characteristics of ghosts that are noticed repeatedly and may be said to constitute their natures, at least insofar as we, the living, are able to understand them. One is that they usually haunt one place on the earth, often a dwelling place. Haunted houses are common. Another is that they customarily repeat the same action, or series of actions, almost as though they are supernatural recordings that are played from time to time for the living able to perceive them.

Ghosts seldom engage in conversations with the living. If they notice the living at all, it may be only with a kind of low malice, suggesting that they have a very limited consciousness. When they do talk, they sometimes express surprise when told that they are dead. They may appear to be confused or in some sort of semi-trance condition.

On rare occasions a ghost may seem completely corporeal, but most often they are nebulous, translucent, and semi-formed, and pass through tables, doors, and walls with no hindrance. They are able to do so because they are inhabitants of the astral level, not the physical level, and are composed of astral substance. There is nothing physical in the makeup of a ghost, but at times it seems they are able to affect physical objects, including human flesh.

Ghosts have been known to kiss the living, or to strike them so hard that the blow leaves a bruise. These seemingly physical events may be explained as subjective on the part of the human beings involved. They feel the kiss, but that does not mean there was an actual physical kiss upon their lips. As for the bruising, it is well known that belief can cause astonishing changes in the body of the believer. The best example of this is the stigmata, the wounds of Christ that sometimes appear on the hands and feet of impressionable individuals. The strong conviction that a blow has been struck, and the very real sensation of such a blow, can cause a bruise to appear on the skin, even when there was no actual physical contact.

There are many reports of ghosts moving objects around, but their power to affect the physical world in this direct way usually appears to be slight. The exception is when ghost sightings are accompanied by poltergeist events. These most often occur in the presence of young children who are approaching puberty or in puberty. Awakening but suppressed sexual energy in the children appears to be connected with the physical manifestations. It seems that ghosts, or spirits assumed to be ghosts, can tap into this sexual energy and use it in some unknown way to move objects, start fires, and create other physical happenings.

The presence of a ghost is sometimes indicated by a sudden coolness on the surface of the skin that closely resembles a light, chill draft. I have often felt this myself, and I can testify from personal experience that the touch of a spirit resembles a cool draft so exactly that it would be impossible to tell the two events apart. When you feel a chill breeze on your face or body where there is no draft, you may well be feeling the touch of a ghost that is invisible to your eyes.

Most often ghosts have no purpose, but wander the places they haunt, repeating the same series of actions for different observers. A ghost may be seen only once, but some famous ghosts have been seen by hundreds of people over a span of centuries. Sometimes they attempt to communicate with the living, usually with a family member or close friend. On rare occasions they are malicious and try to cause harm to the living. Their levels of manifestation, and the power they are able to project to the perceptions of living human beings, varies greatly from ghost to ghost.

Not only human ghosts but also the ghosts of animals, and even at times the ghosts of vehicles such as horse-drawn carriages or trains, have been observed. Some persons have even reported seeing ghostly houses, which they mistook for physical structures, but which were not there when they returned later for a second look.

It seems likely that the majority of apparitions are mere psychic or astral recordings of past events that replay themselves at odd times for the perceptions of chance observers. However, a minority of ghosts are much more self-aware and are capable of causing harm to those who injudiciously seek them out. Such persistent ghosts become famous over the centuries and are not to be trifled with. They are not of the same kind as the pale shades that mechanically perform tasks without noticing that they are being watched.

It is my own speculation that such self-aware ghosts are of a different class entirely and are actually spiritual beings who have assumed as their own the identity of a person who has died. They take on this false identity in the way a hermit crab will put on the shell of another sea creature as its own. So closely does such a spirit identify with the dead person that it actually believes itself to be the dead person, and no amount of argument will convince it otherwise. Some of these spirits are malicious, some are hungry, and some are powerful. Although the average shade is harmless, these ghostly changelings most certainly are not.

DEMONS

Which brings us to the subject of demons. What is a demon? In a specific theological sense, a demon is believed to be a fallen angel, one of the army of Lucifer that fought at his side in the war in heaven, and as a punishment was cast down with him into an abyss beneath the earth—or as some believe, onto the surface of the earth. In a more general sense, a demon is a very powerful and malicious spiritual being that seeks to harm living human beings.

Do they exist? Yes, they do. We apply the same reasoning that we used for vampires, werewolves, and ghosts. Countless honest, average people have seen demons over the centuries, and have experienced the effects of their malice. Why would they lie? Some of them might make up such stories, but not all of them. Consequently, we must assume that they saw something demonic, or at least that they believed themselves to have witnessed something demonic.

If we dismiss the notion that demonic spirits can materialize physically in our material world, then what these witnesses perceived was not physical, even though it seemed physical to them and even though it may have manifested physical effects. As I have mentioned, a spirit can seem to be physically present, with a body of flesh, but this is an illusion. The demon itself is not an illusion—it is quite real, although incorporeal—but when it puts on what seems to be a body of flesh, the body of flesh is an illusion of the senses.

Demons may torment human beings in two ways—obsession and possession. *Obsession* is a term for persistent, repeated sensory perceptions of a spirit. When a person sees or hears or feels the touches of a spirit time after time, and that spirit refuses to stop appearing to the individual, it is obsession. Obsession is an external event—at least, it appears to the person suffering from it to be something outside the body. The obsessing demon, if a demon chooses to obsess a human, will come regularly to vex that person by pinching them, slapping them, whispering in their ear, making faces at them, tripping them, causing foul smells, and so on.

Demon obsession is dangerous mainly because it can cause madness, or a depression so deep that it results in violent acts or in suicide. My own belief is that many of the inexplicable murders and other violent crimes that seem to have no motive are motivated by demonic obsession. Such criminals will sometimes say that a voice told them to commit the crime. The Son of Sam murderer, David Berkowitz, asserted that he was ordered to kill by his neighbor's pet German shepherd, Sam. The dog—or rather, a demon that used the dog as its earthly vehicle—repeatedly commanded Berkowitz to commit murders, until his will to resist was weakened and he acquiesced.

Here is part of a letter Berkowitz wrote to the New York Police Department on April 17, 1977. The letter was left at the scene of a murder:

> I am deeply hurt by your calling me a weman-hater [*sic*]. I am not. But I am a monster. I am the "Son of Sam." I am a little brat. When father Sam gets drunk he gets mean. He beats our family. Sometimes he ties me up to the back of the house. Other times he locks me in the garage. Sam loves to drink blood. "Go out and kills" commands father Sam. Behind our house some rest. Mostly young—raped and slaughtered— their blood drained—just bones now. Pap Sam keeps me locked in the attic too. I can't get out but I look out the attick window and watch the world go by. I feel like an outsider. I am on a different wavelength then everybody else—programmed to kill.[2]

Demonic *possession* occurs when a demon inhabits and takes over the body of a human being, using that body for its own physical body. The human consciousness is displaced at these times. Most often the possessed individual has no awareness of what the demon does while in control of the body, but sometimes the possessed person retains a dim, dreamlike awareness of what is going on but has no will power to stop the things his or her body is doing.

There may be a fine line that is difficult to define between obsession and possession. We see it in the case of Berkowitz. He was aware of what he did, so he was not in the grip of full demonic possession, but he felt himself helpless to resist. He was "locked in the attic"—the attic being his own brain, able to look out the window and watch what was happening, but not able to stop it.

It is my belief that demons have committed murders when in possession of human bodies. Fortunately for humanity, such murderous spiritual beings are uncommon. Possession in itself is not a rare event, contrary to popular belief. Possession happens frequently to those who are mediumistic by nature and may happen to almost everyone from time to time, but the spirits taking control of our bodies are not malicious, and they do no harm either to us or to others around us. When we are possessed, we experience only a gap in time, and usually we assume that we have been daydreaming. Such possessions only become impossible to ignore when the spirit in control of our body commits some act of violence or destruction.

There is a religious belief that in some way demons are prevented from causing direct harm to human beings. The notion is that a higher power prohibits such interference in human affairs. It would be comforting, were it so. My own view is that at times demons do have the freedom to harm either those they possess, or others near them, by using the possessed body as an instrument of violence or murder. Exactly what principles apply—why demons possess one individual and not another—remain unknown. It is fortunate that cases of outright demonic possession are so rare.

If you wish to chill your blood, take time to reflect that vampires, werewolves, ghosts, and demons all exist, on a plane that is not the physical, but is only one step removed from our physical world. At certain times of day, such as twilight, or on certain dates in the year, such as Halloween, these beings can more easily cross over into our reality and be perceived by us, and interact with us. Those who experience them directly seldom doubt their reality ever again.

NOTES

1. Genesis 9:4.

2. Christianson and Levine, pp. 93–94.

7

Guerilla Divination

Divination can be done with the simplest of readily available household or personal items, or even with "found" objects picked up in whatever place you happen to be. Formal and elaborate systems of divination such as astrology or the Tarot are excellent tools for probing the unknown or the future, but they can be difficult to learn, and for this reason many people find them intimidating. It is fortunate that they are not necessary.

Sortilege, or divination by the fall of lots, is a simple technique that requires only a knowledge of a few basic principles, which may be applied to a wide range of objects and conditions. With these principles in mind, you can create your own personal method of divination anywhere, from virtually anything that comes to hand.

In order to extract meaning from the random fall of lots, it is necessary to apply a set of rules. These rules separate order out from chaos. They define boundaries and characterize those bounded areas with different qualities.

We do the same thing when we play a field game such as baseball. The game would be impossible to play unless both sides agreed to follow a pre-established set of game rules delineating what is permissible and defining the meaning of various events.

In games, the rules often seem quite arbitrary, but in divination they must be based on sound esoteric principles, if the divination is to have meaning on the material and spiritual levels of our lives.

Here I will create a completely new method of divination, as a way of explaining some of the basic rules of sortilege—rules that applied every bit as much to the ancient Egyptians, Babylonians, and Greeks as they do to us. This method is completely workable and effective. Do not be fooled by its simplicity—results as detailed and penetrating as those achieved by more formal divination methods are possible, because this method is in harmony with the universal principles of sortilege.

Heads and tails

We will call the method *coin divination*. You will need a penny, a nickel, a dime, and a quarter. That is all you will need. Those using a different form of coinage from that of the United States can achieve the same results with any four different coins—just substitute them in place of the penny, nickel, dime, and quarter.

Examine the penny. It has two sides, and they can easily be distinguished from each other. One side has a human head in profile. For this reason it is referred to as the "heads" side when the simplest of all sortilege techniques is used to decide a question—the coin toss. The other side is conventionally called the "tails" side of the coin, on the presumption that if one side is the head, the opposite side must be the tail of the beast.

It does not matter what is on the obverse and reverse of the coin, only that the two sides are different, because when the coin is randomized by dropping it onto a surface, one of two possibilities will result. We can apply this to any object with two different sides that are equally likely to land uppermost—a flat rock, a button, a chip of wood. Coins are convenient because they are quite regular and well balanced.

The simplest possible answer to a given question is yes or no, but a coin toss can decide between any pair of opposites—left or right, now or later, stop or start, his or hers, win or lose, true or false, and so on. Moreover, any object that falls in two ways can be used to make this determination.

As the first rule of our new system of divination, we will make heads signify positive or helpful influences, and tails signify negative or hindering influences. If heads turns up in the divination, it should generally be looked upon as a good sign, but if tails turns up, it should be taken as unfortunate, in the context of whatever question or circumstance is being investigated.

Now take a look at the other three coins. Each has two sides, so we already know that when heads turns up for any of these coins, it is a good omen, but when tails turns up, it is a bad omen.

What else do you notice about the coins? They are all of different sizes. The dime is the smallest; the penny is the second in size; the nickel is third; and the quarter is the largest of the four. We can use this size difference as the basis for another principle of divination and say that the size determines the relative importance of the fall of the coin. The way in which the quarter falls is more important than the way the nickel falls, because the quarter is a larger coin than the nickel. By the same token, the way the nickel falls is more important than the way the penny falls, because the nickel is bigger than the penny. Similarly, the fall of the penny is more significant than the fall of the dime.

You might object that a dime is worth more than a penny, so the dime should be of greater importance. But remember, we are not using the coins as money; we are using them as objects for sortilege. What is important is their physical appearance and the differences between them, not their abstract and arbitrary monetary value.

Since the quarter is larger, its heads is more weighty or important than the heads of the dime, which is smaller. A cast of the coins that results in the quarter falling heads up, but the other coins showing tails, is not so bad as a cast that results in the dime landing heads but the other three coins, tails.

Two heads and two tails indicate a stalemate or lack of resolution in the question under inquiry. Three heads is generally favorable, three tails generally unfavorable. Four heads is almost certainly an indicator of a positive outcome, and four tails is just as likely to show an unfortunate result.

The quarter falling heads can largely balance the negative influence of two smaller coins falling tails, but the quarter falling tails tends to weight the reading pessimistically, unless the other three coins are all heads.

COPPER AND SILVER

What other difference is there among the coins? The penny is coppery in color, but the other coins are silvery in color. This creates a division in the coins of one and three—one brown coin and three shiny coins. The single coin that is different may be assigned the role of significator, and be used to signify the querent (person asking the question) in the divination. The placement of the penny in the casting of the coins gives insight into the situation of the querent in the circumstances surrounding the question.

The fall of the quarter is usually the most important matter in the question, relative to the querent; the fall of the nickel a matter of intermediary importance; and the fall of the dime the least important matter in question, from the querent's perspective.

The three silvery coins that are apart from the coin representing the querent may be assigned the three parts of any trinity. The most obvious trinity is that of the family— father, mother, and child. The quarter represents the father, because the father is traditionally head of the family, and the quarter is the largest of these three coins; the nickel represents the mother, second in the trinity of the family; the dime represents the child.

I should mention here that when we deal in magic, we get the best results when we use age-old traditional symbolism and associations. Modern socially correct viewpoints may conflict with these traditional values, but we use the traditional meanings because the subconscious mind is conservative and traditional when it comes to symbols and archetypes. In occult symbolism the father remains the head of the family, even if modern social opinion would like to do away with this paternal primacy.

If you feel very strongly that such traditional symbolism is incorrect, by all means change it in your own divination to suit your convictions—but be aware that you subconscious mind is probably not nearly as socially aware as your conscious mind.

The quarter is, in a more general sense, the authority figure in the matter of the question—the leader, the boss, the teacher, the law-giver, the maker and enforcer of rules. It is also the primary factor, the center around which the rest revolve, the support for the rest of the matter under investigation. These meanings descend from the traditional archetypal role of the father.

The nickel is in a general sense the caregiver in the matter of the question, the supporting ally, the understanding confidant, the helpmate, the giver of advice and sympathy, the friend. It is also the secondary factor, the support for the center without which the center would collapse, the necessary but overshadowed aspect of the matter. These meanings stem from the archetypal role of the mother.

The dime is in a general sense the irresponsible figure in the matter of the question, the trickster, the weak member of the team, an uninformed or unreliable person. It is also the unpredictable factor, the potential monkey wrench, the matter that requires watching, care, and attention; the potential problem. These meanings derive from the archetypal role of the child.

CASTING PATTERNS

Having differentiated the coins according to their obvious physical differences, we can look at the patterns they make when they are cast. Patterns formed by lots are of the highest importance in sortilege, because they convey so much information. In some forms of sortilege, individual patterns can acquire an arbitrary meaning, but here we will look only at the general principles of pattern interpretation that may be applied to all forms of divination by lots.

Two coins touching indicates two connected factors that are jointly affecting the question. One coin lying on top, or partially on top, of another coin shows that one factor is dominating the factor to which it is linked.

The distance separating coins indicates distance in time separating them. Silvery coins nearest the penny, which is the significator, show factors that are near in the future, but silvery coins farther away from the penny show factors that are more remote in the future. The significator is the querent in the context of the question, so the other three coins are interpreted from the perspective of the penny, as they relate to the penny.

Two coins near together but not touching suggest two factors, or two individuals, that are converging but may not yet be linked. The coins may stand for physical things, for ideas, or for individuals, that fall under their general categories.

Coins arranged in a line indicate a chain of events. If the line is somewhat straight, the outcome will be forceful and direct. If it is curved, the outcome will be deceptive, and possibly an illusion. If the line is a zigzag, the outcome will be less direct and somewhat confused. These patterns need not be perfect. The coins are never going to fall into a perfectly straight line, or will do so only rarely. Attention must be given as to whether the coins make a line that is more straight than curved, more regular than jagged.

The position of the penny in this line of coins shows the position of the querent relative to other factors in the matter under inquiry. For example, the penny separated from the quarter by the dime gives the indication that a rogue factor or individual is preventing clear communication or action between the querent and the heart of the matter. On the other hand, the nickel between the penny and quarter indicates that a friend or helper is assisting communication between the querent and the leader or central factor. The nickel helps the penny, but the dime hinders the penny.

When the three silvery coins fall tightly around the penny, the indication is that the querent will be pressured by the factors they represent, to a greater or lesser degree, depending on how closely the other coins hem in the penny.

If the penny falls a long distance from the other three coins, which cluster together, the indication is that the querent will seek to distance himself or herself from the matter of the reading, or that the querent feels detached from the matter.

When three coins form a triangular shape with roughly equal sides, there is general harmony or agreement among the factors represented by those coins. This does not necessarily mean that they are working together, but rather than they are on the same wavelength, and share a common awareness or understanding.

When the three silver coins form a regular triangle around the penny, situated roughly at the center, this is auspicious, because it indicates harmony of forces. The triangle is harmonious. However, there is some danger of stagnation in this pattern, since the harmony among the factors represented by the silvery coins may work against the aggressive action of the querent, by softening it or delaying it. The difference between being supported by the three surrounding silvery coins, and being stifled and oppressed by them, is only one of degree.

If the four coins form a rough cross, we can determine significant information from the pattern, depending on which arm of the cross holds the penny. When the penny is at the head of the cross, the querent is in control of the situation; when the penny is at the foot of the cross, the querent is in a subservient position with regard to the matter under question; when the penny is on the right arm of the cross (the right side of the divination surface, from the diviner's perspective), the querent must use reason and persuasion to achieve a good outcome; when the penny is on the left arm of the cross, more forceful action is required, but the querent most take care not to give in to anger or resort to violence, even if the temptation is strong.

How do we get these meanings from the cross? They are not arbitrary. The head is always a symbol of leadership or mastery. It is the ruler of the body, the seat of the will. By contrast, the opposite foot is the place of submission—servants and slaves kneel at the feet of their overlords. The arms are the appendages of action and work—in a symbolic sense the right arm the side of reason and order, the opposite left arm the side of emotion and imbalance.

Method of working

When casting the coins, the diviner must have the question clearly in mind, and must understand it. The coins should be shaken in the cupped hands, or in a small vessel such as a cup, to randomize them, while the diviner holds the question in mind. Then they are cast with care onto a convenient surface, in such a way that they do not roll a great distance. The best surface for casting is soft, such as a rug or blanket. It allows the coins to bounce and roll somewhat, but dampens their movement so that they do not roll too far away and spoil the cast.

Casting lots, such as the four coins of this present method, is something of an art in itself. It requires practice. You must cast the lots so that they fall freely, but with only so much force as is required to give them a little separation. Ideally, the cast lots should cover an area little larger than a dinner plate.

Sometimes one coin may get away and roll a short distance. This is acceptable, as long as the rogue coin does not travel more than a couple of feet. If the coins scatter too widely, or if one or more of them rolls a long distance, the reading must be aborted, and the coins cast again.

In making this kind of cast, I like to cup my two hands together, shake up the lots between my hollowed palms, and then open my hands quickly but gently around a foot over a soft surface, so that the lots fall directly downward onto the surface. This gives a good separation and random fall, but is gentle enough that the lots do not fly in all directions. In my own work, I often cast rune dice in this way, with good results, but the technique also applies to coins.

The original form of divination I have described in this chapter does not exist anywhere but here. I created it while writing this essay to illustrate how the general principles of sortilege, and divination as a whole, may be applied to any set of simple objects to yield a workable system of fortune telling. Once you know the principles, you can divine anywhere, with almost anything.

8

Sensory Metaphors

I intend to discuss here the nature of reality. The concept of real and unreal held by a magician is quite different from that of the average person. Those of us who work magic for any length of time are invariably forced to change our understanding of reality, and the deeper we venture into the philosophy of magic, the greater our sense of what is real diverges from that of society at large. I will try to avoid being too abstract in this essay, but some grasp of the magical perception of reality is required in order to comprehend certain aspects of the occult, such as the true nature of spiritual beings.

When we are born, that part of our brain that holds our identity is a blank slate, waiting to be written on by the impressions of our physical senses. As we age, we acquire more and more experiences, and these are stored as memories. We are the sum of our memories. Take them away, as happens sometimes in severe strokes, and we cease to exist. Our body continues, but it is no more than a physical shell. It is not who we are. Who we are is undifferentiated super-consciousness, acting through the filter of our various levels of memory, which shape and define that consciousness, limiting it into what we know as our personal identity.

We can never conceive anything apart from the input of our senses. That is the tragedy of the human experience. Try to conceive of a thing that is not based on your prior sense impressions and you will see that it is so. You cannot do it. If you think of a monster that has never existed, you will see that it is built up of familiar parts that you have learned about through your senses—skin, teeth, legs, eyes, ears, a tail. It will be certain colors, will emit sounds, will have a distinctive smell, be rough or smooth to the touch. We simply cannot imagine anything other than sense impressions.

Even when we try to imagine completely abstract things, we can only hold them in our minds by translating them into familiar sensory models. This is the reason we cannot picture higher dimensions of space, but must use three-dimensional models to suggest them. It is a fundamental, inherent limitation of human consciousness, part of the very nature of what we are.

Even more startling the first time it is understood is the realization that the entire universe that we know and everything it contains exists only in our mind. That is not to say that another level of the universe might not exist apart and independent of our awareness, but if so we can never know anything about it. That is the key insight. We are prisoners of our own perceptions. Our consciousness is based on perceptual information, and the universe for us exists only in our mind.

You may have heard about Plato's cave. The Greek philosopher Plato wrote in his dialogue *The Republic* that human beings are like prisoners, chained in a cave, who sit with their backs to the fire and perceive nothing of what passes behind them apart from the shadows that play across the cave wall. The cave is human consciousness. The light from the fire is our senses. The shadows are the things we build up in our minds based on our sense impressions. All we know consciously are the shadows. The moving shadows on the wall constitute our reality.

However, the cave is not all we are. In our higher natures, we transcend its limits. Sometimes, beings from outside the cave of sense impressions interact with our awareness. We call them gods, angels, spirits, ghosts, fairies, demons, aliens, and countless other names that attempt to define them in a way that our minds can handle. These beings from outside our perceptual reality are faced with a quandary. They exist beyond our senses, and we can only understand things of our senses, so how are they to reach our awareness?

They do it by using a technique that I have named *sensory metaphors*. A sensory metaphor is nonsensory information that has been translated into sensory information. The mind is incredibly versatile, despite its inherent limitations. It is capable of translating one sensory input into another sensory input under extraordinary conditions such as illness, or a head injury, or under the influence of mind-altering drugs such as LSD. We can, under certain conditions, hear colors, for example, or see sounds, or even taste concepts. One sensory input can substitute its information for another input from a different sense.

This translation of sensory perceptions from one sense to another happens as a normal part of life for those who are blessed with a very rare condition known as synesthesia, which causes them to smell sounds, or hear colors. Or they may taste colors, or smell them. I say blessed rather than cursed, because who among us would not like to be able to see music as a dancing rainbow?

But the mind is even more versatile. It can process information that has no sensory base at all into sensory data, thus allowing us to become aware of its existence, and to consider it by analogy. That is to say, we can never consider the super-sensory data itself because it lies beyond the reach of our consciousness, but we can contemplate the sensory metaphors of that unreachable data, in the same way we can represent and manipulate the higher dimensions of space with three-dimensional models.

An example of this is the perception of auras. Auras—the colored halos that are seen by some psychics to surround the bodies of human beings—are not a translation of another physical sense impression into a visual impression, but are the manifestation of something that lies beyond the physical senses in a form that appears to be a visual sense impression.

When an angel appears to a human being, it has no physical reality. It cannot be seen, heard, touched, smelled, or tasted. You may object that reports of angels throughout human history record that they appeared as physical beings. Often angels are said to walk among us in the guise of ordinary human beings who can be touched. Women have even made love to angels.

True enough. It was not the angel that was perceived, but the sensory metaphor generated by the angel, which in its essence exists in a realty that lies beyond our capacity to comprehend. Only because the angel has generated a sensory metaphor of itself do we even know that an angel is present. If the angel wishes to communicate with us, it must express itself in a way we can hold in our thoughts and imprint on our memories. It must become sensory data in our minds, even though that data never passes through any of the physical avenues of our senses.

Unless a spirit generates a sensory metaphor of itself, we continue unaware of it even though it may be very near. It is sometimes said that the world throngs with spirits of all kinds, but that we remain unconscious of their existence. This is true. To become real to us, a spirit must engage our mind on our own level of understanding.

Sensory metaphors of a simple kind arise spontaneously under unusual conditions. When we see a ghost, we do not actually see anything at all—rather, we have the impression in our minds of seeing. The true nature of the ghost, which we cannot perceive directly because it lies beyond our senses, is translated into a sensory metaphor. Usually this takes the form of a visual image. It may be indistinct or translucent. Sometimes the ghost takes the sensory metaphor of a sound or series of sounds, sometimes an odor, sometimes a touch, and only very rarely it appears as a taste. Ghosts can simulate or imitate more than one sense at a time, and we may both hear and see a ghost, or feel the touch of a ghost and simultaneously smell a distinct odor such as cigar smoke or perfume.

Complex spirits, who have a more developed intelligence, seem able to at least in part control the sensory metaphors that we perceive, so that they can present themselves in whatever way they think is to their advantage in dealing with us, and if necessary, change their appearance. You have no doubt heard of demons summoned by magicians into the triangle of evocation who come first in a frightening and horrible form in an attempt to intimidate the magician, but when commanded by the authority of names of power, will put on more pleasing forms in order to converse with the magician.

Spirits are not in their essence the sensory metaphors that represent them. They become those forms in their dealings with us, in order to be able to make us aware of their existence and communicate with us, and to us they are those forms, just as to us a human being is the body that he or she inhabits. But apart from our consciousness the essence of the spirit is a thing we simply are not capable of comprehending. It is what lies outside Plato's cave and we can never turn our head to look directly at it, because it is not within our capacity to do so.

The doctrine of sensory metaphors explains many mysteries about the nature of spirits. For example, why a spirit can seem completely and physically real to one individual, yet pass unperceived by another individual who is nearby. It explains why a spirit can be touched yet cannot be photographed. Whether or not genuine spirit or ghost photographs exist is a matter for debate. My own firm conviction is that such photographs do not exist. A being that cannot be perceived directly by human senses cannot register on photographic light sensors, because in a strictly material sense, it is not there at all. Yet the sensory metaphor of that spirit can seem completely real and present to whomever it is presented.

All the tricks of capricious spirits become understandable. Fairies were noted for their fairy feasts, which would be there one moment and gone the next, and for their fairy gold, which after being given would turn to straw or vanish away completely. The doctrine of sensory metaphors explains the sudden appearance and vanishing of spiritual beings of various types, how they can seem material yet pass through solid walls or doors, how they can appear to turn to smoke or mist, how they can transmute themselves into the shapes of beasts.

Sensory metaphors should not be thought of as completely arbitrary and ephemeral. True, they are not real in the narrow sense that our sensory impressions of physical objects are considered real, yet they often express accurately the nature of the spirit that adopts them. When a spirit retains a sensory metaphor for long enough, it effectively becomes the spirit, just as we are our collection of thoughts and memories. A goddess conceived for thousands of years in a certain form, with specific characteristics, becomes that being permanently, insofar as anything in this ever-shifting universe can be said to have permanence. The name given to the goddess becomes the name of that spirit. Aphrodite is Aphrodite; she is not merely a spirit pretending to be Aphrodite.

A spirit that manifests over a long period as the sensory metaphor of Abraham Lincoln, for example, may truly believe itself to be the spirit of the dead president. And who is to say it is not correct? Its identity is based on the same motivations, the same beliefs, the same memory of experiences, that

formed the personality of Lincoln. If it is not the actual spiritual essence of Lincoln's soul, assuming such a separate and
discrete essence to exist, then it is a clone of that essence. Perhaps the spirit is even able to tap into some higher aspect of
Lincoln's being, a kind of divine template of Lincoln that is
stored in the akashic records.

The control higher spirits have over sensory metaphors
should cause us to be thankful most spirits are benevolent.
The ability to control what we perceive through our physical
senses gives these spirits, at least potentially, the power of
life and death over us. We have all had sensory tricks played
on us by spiritual beings, although many of you reading
this may not have realized it. We put down our car keys,
turn round to do something, and when we turn back, the
keys are gone. We search the table they were on, the room,
the whole house without finding them, and the next day
when we pass the table, there are the keys, sitting in plain
sight just where we left them. This kind of thing happens
so often, it scarcely causes us to think about it. However,
if we considered the matter, we would realize that someone has been playing games with our perceptions. How else
could we fail to see what was in plain sight the whole time
we looked for it?

Poltergeists play with human perceptions all the time.
This is the primary way they work their tricks. Usually this
manipulation of the senses is coupled with the spirit possession of a human being, who unwittingly acts as their
physical agent to move things or perform various physical
tasks. Much of poltergeist phenomena is physical, but much
of it only appears to be physical, but is actually composed
of sensory metaphors. For example, everyone in the house

may suddenly hear a deafening clap of thunder, yet no one in the neighboring houses will have heard a thing, because the thunder was not an actual sound, but merely the metaphor of thunder that existed only in the minds of those who heard it.

There seems to be some principle of nature that prevents spirits from killing or injuring human beings often and in large numbers through the malicious manipulation of our senses. It does happen on rare occasions, but the demons that do it are outlaws or renegades that have in some way stepped over the bounds of normal spirit behavior. Apparently there are no laws against playing with us, annoying us, or terrifying us, other than the general laws of good manners and good taste, and some spirits delight to do these things, though what their motives may be is a matter for conjecture. Maybe they are amusing themselves at out expense, or maybe they derive some personal benefit from generating strong emotions of anger, frustration, or fear. Perhaps these strong emotions nourish lower spirits, and it is for this reason that they manipulate our senses in order to generate these emotions.

It is my view that the concept of sensory metaphors is essential to achieve a useful understanding of the nature of human-spirit interaction in the 21st century. The old mechanical notions of spirit nature simply will not serve our purposes in this quantum age. We cannot weigh and photograph spiritual beings, and it is high time we got over this simplistic understanding of our reality. All that we know is conditioned by our senses, but it is not limited to our senses. Our reality contains higher levels beyond the sensory, and higher-dimensional beings with which we can interact, but only in a secondary way, by a process of translation that models the higher levels of reality in sensory forms that our mind is capable of handling. We should be thankful that our minds are so versatile, they allow this translation to occur, for without it we would know nothing of spirits, not even that they exist.

9

Order of the Tarot Trumps

Origins of the Tarot

The Tarot has been a central part of the Western esoteric tradition since 1781, when Antoine Court de Gébelin (1728–84) made it a topic of interest by including two analytical essays on the subject in volume 8 of his nine volume encyclopedia, *Monde primitif*, the separate volumes of which were published between the years 1773 and 1782. One of the essays was written by de Gébelin himself, and the other by Louis-Raphaël-Lucréce de Fayolle, comte de Mellet (1727–1804). My English translation of both essays was published in the online magazine *Rending the Veil*.

Court de Gébelin believed that the Tarot was Egyptian in its origins, that its 22 picture cards, known as the trumps, were based on the 22 letters of an Egyptian alphabet related to the Hebrew alphabet, and that it had been spread through-out the world by gypsies, who were thought by many scholars at the time to have come from Egypt. In all of these particu-lars he was quite wrong. Even so, his essay exerted a profound influence over the esoteric interpretation of the Tarot in France during the following century, through the writings of such occultists as Alphonse Louis Constant (1810–75), who wrote under the pen name Éliphas Lévi, and Gérard Encausse (1865–1916), who was known as Papus. From France this bias made its way into the beliefs and practices of various esoteric schools, such as the Hermetic Order of the Golden Dawn in England and the Builders of the Adytum in America.

The true origins of the Tarot are, on the surface at least, quite mundane. They are known in a general way, although no one can say exactly when the Tarot was invented, or by whom. It first appeared in northern Italy around 1425 as a card game for bored and wealthy Italian aristocrats. The game was called the game of Tarot, and was a trick-taking game somewhat similar to bridge. It is still played today, and it is why the picture cards of the Tarot are known as trumps. The inspiration of its inventor was to add the 22 trumps to a set of 56 cards that was very similar to the com-mon decks of playing cards in use in Europe at the time the game of Tarot was invented. More than one kind of Tarot deck came into being in the early decades of the 15th cen-tury, and the number of cards varied, but the Tarot quickly settled into its present pattern of 22 trumps and 56 minor cards in four suits.

Court de Gébelin may have been mistaken in his belief that the Tarot had an ancient and lofty origin among the priest class of Egypt, but he was not wrong to assign it a

profound esoteric significance. Even today, the Tarot speaks
to those who study it, using the language of symbolism. It
became the central device for the system of occultism of
the Hermetic Order of the Golden Dawn, a secret Rosicrucian society established in London in 1888. The leaders of
the Golden Dawn based much of their interpretations of
the cards on the work of the French occultists of the 19th
century. Via the teachings of the Golden Dawn, the Tarot
correspondences used in that occult order were spread
throughout the world, and are still the prevalent Tarot correspondences today.

Tarot correspondences

Tarot correspondences are the sets of esoteric symbols associated with the Tarot. Each card is linked to symbols of occult
forces, or names of spiritual beings, drawn from various
sources such as alchemy, astrology, numerology, the Kabbalah, and geomancy. The links are more numerous in the
case of the Tarot trumps, which bear images rich in meaning. For example, the trump the Magician is linked in the
Golden Dawn system of magic with the Hebrew letter Beth,
the number one, the astrological planet Mercury, the twelfth
path on the Kabbalistic Tree of Life, and with the ox, a beast
associated esoterically with the Hebrew letter of this trump.
Correspondences provide bridges to other correspondences.
Because the trump the Magician is associated with the planet
Mercury, it is also linked with the angel of Mercury, Raphael;
the Intelligence of Mercury, Tiriel; and the Spirit of Mercury,
Taphthartharath.

Since the occult correspondences for each Tarot trump
are connected by various associative bridges, to manipulate

any of them is to gain a measure of control over all of them. This works on the basis of the same general magical principle that governs the well-known magical law of contagion, which states that a thing that was once in physical contact with someone is still in touch with that person on some deep level, and therefore manipulating the object causes influence to be exerted on the person it formerly touched. The associations connecting the forces and beings that form the occult correspondences for a Tarot card are like links in a chain. Move one link, and they all rattle.

The Golden Dawn Tarot correspondences are rooted in Court de Gébelin's casual observation that there are 22 trumps, and 22 Hebrew letters. The French occultists such as Éliphas Lévi had already placed the trumps on the Hebrew alphabet by the time the leader of the Golden Dawn, S. L. MacGregor Mathers (1854–1918), came to create the Golden Dawn system of esoteric Tarot correspondences. Mathers did not adopt exactly the same relationship as that used by Lévi, and that difference and others like it are what this essay is all about, but he followed the same general principle. Each Hebrew letter has various esoteric associations. By linking the Hebrew letter to a Tarot trump, those associations can be transferred to the trump.

Since, in modern Western magic, the Tarot trumps derive their correspondences through the Hebrew letters, it is obviously a matter of great significance which Hebrew letter is linked to which trump. The ordering of the Hebrew letters is not open to reinterpretation, but has been established and accepted for thousands of years. However, the ordering of the Tarot trumps does not have such an ancient or well-established history. Indeed, the earliest Tarot decks were unnumbered. The sequence of the Tarot trumps was a matter of oral tradition. It was passed on between those who played the game of Tarot, and it appears that in the decades following the invention of the Tarot, there was more than one accepted ordering for the trumps, as pointed out by the authors of the modern work on the history of the Tarot *A Wicked Pack of Cards*:

> But, when the pack was first standardised, the subjects of the trump cards were standardised, too; they were at first everywhere the same.
>
> Somewhat surprisingly, however, they were not everywhere arranged in the same order. The variations in order were not a later development, but must have occurred from the earliest moment when Tarot cards were known in the principal original centres of their use—Milan, Ferrara, Bologna, and Florence.[1]

Trump sequence of the Marseilles Tarot

We need not go into the earliest sequences of the trumps, some of which are uncertain, but may begin with Court de Gébelin, since it is with his Tarot essay of 1781 that the esoteric history of the Tarot really begins, at least in a documented manner—for there was an esoteric tradition of the Tarot in use in France in the late 18th century, when de Gébelin published his essay, but exactly what it taught, we cannot be sure, other than that some of those teachings must be reflected in de Gébelin's essay.

Court de Gébelin accepted the traditional ordering of the trumps of his day, as it was codified in the numbering of the French pack of Tarot cards known as the Tarot of Marseilles. As I mentioned, the earliest Italian Tarot decks were unnumbered, but as early as 1490 card makers in Ferrara, Italy, probably began to place Roman numerals on the trumps, fixing them into a specific sequence.[2] This practice was carried on by the early French card makers. It is uncertain which of the Italian trump sequences was adopted in what came to be known as the Tarot of Marseilles, but it is speculated that it may have been the ordering used by the Tarot card makers of Milan.[3] The Marseilles sequence of trumps, with its original French spellings as they appear on the 1761 pack designed by Nicolas Conver, is as follows:

I. Le Bateleur (The Juggler)

II. La Papesse (The Female Pope)

III. L'Imperatrice (The Empress)

IIII. L' Empereur (The Emperor)

V. Le Pape (The Pope)

VI. L'Amovrevx (The Lover)

VII. Le Chariot (The Chariot)

VIII. La Justice (Justice)

VIIII. L'Hermite (The Hermit)

X. La Rove De Fortvne (The Wheel of Fortune)

XI. La Force (Strength)

XII. Le Pendu (The Hanged Man)

XIII. — (Death)

XIIII. Temperance (Temperance)

XV. Le Diable (The Devil)

XVI. La Maison Diev (The House of God)

XVII. L' Etoille (The Star)

XVIII. La Lune (The Moon)

XVIIII. Le Soleil (The Sun)

XX. Le Jugement (Judgement)

XXI. Le Monde (The World)

Le Mat (The Fool)

A few points are to be noticed. The method of writing Roman numerals is slightly different from the accepted manner of today. Instead of using IV to represent the number four, IIII was used. Sometimes in writing the names of the trumps, the letter *v* was employed where we would put the letter *u* today. The trump L'Amovrevx is usually called the Lovers, but the singular form, the Lover, may be more accurate. It is translated in this way on the trump in the well-known Grimaud Tarot. The trump Death did not have its name written on the face of the card at all, although the title of this card was known to everyone using the Tarot. This was in keeping with the popular superstition that to speak the name of Death was to invoke this dreaded dark angel. The trump the Fool did not bear a number of any kind. The lack of a number derived from the way the Fool was used in the game of Tarot.

TRUMP SEQUENCE OF COURT DE GÉBELIN

Court de Gébelin renamed some of the trumps to give them a more Egyptian flavor, but he retained their Marseilles sequence. It was the usual custom to place the only trump that remained unnumbered, the Fool, at the end of the sequence, following XXI, the World. Court de Gébelin declared that it should be numbered zero, because like the zero of mathematics, it has no value of its own, but only acquires value when added to other cards. This statement exerted profound influence over later occultists who wrote about the Tarot.

Court de Gébelin believed that the trumps should be arranged from highest number to lowest number, in the belief that the Egyptians "began counting from the highest number, going down to the lowest."[4] To interpret the cards correctly, he asserted, they must be examined in this manner. It was on this basis that he felt free to rename the Marseilles trump Judgement, which from its name might be expected to come at the end of the sequence, as Creation, which might be expected to come at or near the beginning. Here are the changed titles that de Gébelin applied to the trumps in their reversed order, followed by their usual Marseilles titles in English:

XXI. Time (The World)
XX. Creation (Judgement)
XIX. The Sun (The Sun)
XVIII. The Nile (The Moon)
XVII. The Dog-Star (The Star)
XVI. Castle of Plutus (The House of God)
XV. Typhon (The Devil)
XIV. Temperance (Temperance)
XIII. Death (Death)
XII. Prudence (The Hanged Man)
XI. Fortitude (Strength)
X. Wheel of Fortune (Wheel of Fortune)
IX. The Sage (The Hermit)
VIII. Justice (Justice)
VII. Osiris Triumphant (The Chariot)
VI. Marriage (The Lovers)
V. Chief Hierophant (The Pope)

IV. The Emperor (The Emperor)

III. The Empress (The Empress)

II. The High Priestess (The Female Pope)

I. Lord of Chance (The Juggler)

0. The Fool (The Fool)

TRUMP SEQUENCE OF THE COMTE DE MELLET

What de Gébelin did not do was make a direct relationship between the trumps and the Hebrew letters. However, it is obvious what arrangement he intended, and indeed, his contributor the comte de Mellet supplied the explicit arrangement that must also have been in de Gébelin's thoughts, and applied the inverted sequence of the trumps to the Hebrew alphabet, with the final numbered trump, XXI the World, on the first letter, Aleph, and the unnumbered trump the Fool, to which de Gébelin gave the zero, on the final letter, Tau.

De Mellet seems to have been the first person to explicitly define a relationship between the trumps and Hebrew letters. He called the Fool by the title Madness, and changed some of the other names of the trumps, although his interpretations are not always exactly like those of de Gébelin. It is evident from his descriptions of the Pope and Popess (Female Pope) that rather than the standard Marseilles pack, he used the Tarot of Besancon, where the Pope is replaced by Jupiter and the Popess by Juno.[5]

Here is his sequence of the trumps on the Hebrew letters, along with the interpretations he gave them, translated into English. The more conventional names for the trumps are placed in parentheses.

XXI. The Universe (The World)—Aleph

XX. Creation of Man (Judgement)—Beth

XIX. Creation of the Sun (The Sun)—Gimel

XVIII. Creation of the Moon (The Moon)—Daleth

XVII. Creation of the Stars (The Star)—He

XVI. House of God (House of God)—Vau

XV. Typhon (The Devil)—Zayin

XIV. Angel of Temperance (Temperance)—Cheth

XIII. Death (Death)—Teth

XII. Prudence (The Hanged Man)—Yod

XI. Strength (Strength)—Kaph

X. Goddess Fortune (Wheel of Fortune)—Lamed

IX. The Sage (The Hermit)—Mem

VIII. Justice (Justice)—Nun

VII. Chariot of War (The Chariot)—Samekh

VI. Choice Between Vice or Virtue (The Lovers)—Ayin

V. The God Jupiter (The Pope)—Pe

IV. The King (The Emperor)—Tzaddi

III. The Queen (The Empress)—Qoph

II. The Goddess Juno (The Female Pope)—Resh

I. The Juggler (The Juggler)—Shin

0. Madness (The Fool)—Tau

Trump sequence of Éliphas Lévi

When Éliphas Lévi brought forth the second volume of his two-part *Dogme et rituel de la haute magie*, published in French in 1855–56, he applied the sequence of the Marseilles trumps to the Hebrew alphabet in its traditional order, but he placed the Fool just before the final numbered trump, on the second-last Hebrew letter. Either he did not understand Court de Gébelin's intention to invert the sequence of trumps, or as seems more likely, he chose to ignore it. He was convinced that the posture of the upper body of the Juggler defined the shape of the first Hebrew letter, Aleph, writing "His body and arms constitute the letter Aleph."[6] This cannot be denied, but since few, if any, of the other figures on the cards resemble Hebrew letters, its significance is questionable. Below are his titles for the picture cards of the Tarot, and his placement of the trumps on the Hebrew letters.

I. The Juggler—Aleph
II. The Female Pope—Beth
III. The Empress—Gimel
IV. The Emperor—Daleth
V. The Pope—He
VI. Vice and Virtue—Vau
VII. Cubic Chariot—Zayin
VIII. Justice—Cheth
IX. Prudence—Teth
X. Wheel of Fortune—Yod
XI. Strength—Kaph
XII. The Hanged Man—Lamed
XIII. Death—Mem
XIV. Temperance—Nun
XV. The Devil—Samekh
XVI. Tower Struck By Lightning—Ayin
XVII. The Blazing Star—Pe
XVIII. The Moon—Tzaddi
XIX. The Sun—Qoph
XX. The Judgement—Resh
0. The Fool—Shin
XXI. Kether—Tau

The title for the final trump in Lévi's sequence, which is usually known as the World or Universe, is drawn from the Kabbalah, the system of occult philosophy of the Jews. Kether, a Hebrew word that means *crown*, is the title for the first and highest emanation of God in the ten-stage process by which the universe was created, according to Kabbalistic doctrine. It is represented symbolically by the image of a crown, and to Lévi's imagination the oval or circular wreath on the trump the Universe must have looked similar to a crown.

The placement of the Fool second from the end of the trump sequence by Lévi had considerable influence on later writers on the Tarot. It is difficult to know how to justify this location for the Fool, which appears to have been put at the end of the trumps in the earliest arrangements of the cards, and was placed at the end of the inverted trump sequence by Court de Gébelin.

The French occultist Jean-Baptiste Pitois (1811–77), known by his pen name Paul Christian, imitated Lévi in this quixotic location of the Fool second from the end of the trumps, when he published his monumental (in size if not in content) work, *Histoire de la Magie*, in 1870.[7] Papus also followed Lévi's lead in his *Tarot of the Bohemians*, first published in 1889, by placing the Fool on the second-last Hebrew letter, Shin, just before the final trump, the World.[8] Neither bothered to justify this location for the Fool.

A. E. Waite also followed Lévi's example and put his Fool second from the end of the trump sequence in his *Pictorial Key to the Tarot*, published in 1910, even though he held it to be incorrect. As a member of the Golden Dawn, Waite was bound by oath not to reveal the occult secrets of that Hermetic order, so he could not present the Golden Dawn sequence for the Tarot trumps, which he believed to be esoterically accurate. He deliberately presented what he knew to be a false arrangement of the trumps.

On the placement of the Fool, Waite wrote:

> Court de Gebelin places it at the head of the whole series as the zero or negative which is presupposed by numeration, and as this is a simpler so also it is a better arrangement. It has been abandoned because in later times the cards have been attributed to the letters of the Hebrew alphabet, and there has been apparently some difficulty about allocating the zero symbol satisfactorily in a sequence of letters all of which signify numbers. In the present reference of the card to the letter Shin, which corresponds to 200, the difficulty or the unreason remains. The truth is that the real arrangement of the cards has never transpired.[9]

This quotation from Waite's *Pictorial Key* is worth examining on several points. He was wrong to state that Court de Gébelin placed the Fool "at the head" of the trumps, since de Gébelin inverted the sequence, making trump XXI the head, and the zero card the Fool the tail. It is true that de Gébelin shifted the Fool from the end to the beginning of the sequence, but then he inverted the sequence, which put the Fool back on the end.

It is curious that Waite did not locate the Fool at the beginning of the trumps. This was the esoteric teaching of the Golden Dawn, so perhaps he felt honor-bound not to do so, lest it be construed as a betrayal of a secret. He felt that he knew the "real arrangement" of the trumps, but also felt that it must remain hidden from profane eyes. So he imitated Lévi, fully aware that Lévi's placement of the Fool made no sense, and stating as much to his readers in his book.

In view of his reluctance to put the Fool at the head of the trumps, it is curious that Waite felt free to invert the places of VIII Justice and XI Strength. This inversion was based on the esoteric teaching of the Golden Dawn, and should have been just as taboo for Waite as the true location of the Fool. In his *Pictorial Key* he made this switch, but did not explain it or justify it to his readers.

TRUMP SEQUENCE OF THE GOLDEN DAWN

The location of the Fool at the head of the trumps, and the inversion in the places and numbers of Justice and Strength, are innovations of S. L. MacGregor Mathers, earthly chief of the Hermetic Order of the Golden Dawn. Around the time the Golden Dawn was establishing its first London temple, in 1888, Mathers and his wife were working on an esoteric Tarot deck. His wife, Moïna, formerly Mina Bergson, sister of famous French philosopher Henri Bergson, was an artist, and it was she who actually painted the designs for the new Tarot. Since she was a psychic who often helped her husband in receiving esoteric teachings from the spiritual leaders of the Golden Dawn, known as the Secret Chiefs, it is safe to assume that she was deeply involved not merely in the design, but also in the esoteric interpretation of the new Golden Dawn Tarot. Indeed, it is quite possible that the composition of the Golden Dawn Tarot owes more to Moïna Mathers than to Samuel Mathers.

The major innovation of the Golden Dawn was the absolute determination that the Fool be placed at the front of the Tarot trumps, before the Juggler, which in the Golden Dawn Tarot was called the Magician. This bumped all the trumps up one Hebrew letter. It created the awkward condition of having a card numbered zero falling on a Hebrew letter with a numerical value of one, and so for the rest of the trumps, each out by one number from its Hebrew letter—or at least, the first ten Hebrew letters, since after the letter Yod the number values of the Hebrew letters become nonconsecutive, increasing by tens, and then hundreds.

This awkwardness becomes less distasteful, from an esthetic point of view, when we realize that the numbers on the trumps are not in any way a part of the trumps. For example, the VII on the trump the Chariot is not attached in any way to this card—it merely indicates the location of this card in the trump sequence. How do we know this? Because originally no Tarot trump was numbered. The trumps are picture cards—their identities are in their pictures. The Roman numerals were applied to the trumps merely as an aid to memory, to ensure that errors were not made in their sequence. The seven on the Seven of Wands is very much a part of that Tarot card—indeed, the greater portion of its identity—but the VII on the trump the Chariot is not a part of that trump, and may be removed without in any way diminishing the meaning of the trump.

The second innovation of the Golden Dawn, the inversion of the locations of Justice and Strength, was dictated by the way Mathers and his wife applied the trumps to the

Hebrew letters. They used as their guide the most ancient of Kabbalistic texts, *Sepher Yetzirah*. In this text, the 22 Hebrew letters are divided into three groups:

3 Mother letters: Aleph, Mem, Shin

7 Double letters: Beth, Gimel, Daleth, Kaph, Pe, Resh, Tau

12 Simple letters: He, Vau, Zayin, Cheth, Teth, Yod, Lamed, Nun, Samekh, Ayin, Tzaddi, Qoph

The Mother letters are associated with three of the four philosophical elements, the Double letters with the seven planets of traditional astrology, and the Simple letters with the twelve signs of the zodiac. In the version of *Sepher Yetzirah* translated by W. Wynn Westcott, a leading member of the Golden Dawn, the placements of the elements and zodiac signs on the letters are explicit, but the placement of the planets is somewhat obscure, and open to various interpretations.

If the Tarot trumps were simply applied in order to the Hebrew letters, with the Fool on the first letter, then the trump VIII Justice would fall on the Simple letter Teth, and XI Strength would fall on the Simple letter Lamed. In the correspondence between the Simple letters and the zodiac signs that is given in *Sepher Yetzirah*, this would put the sign Leo on the trump Justice, and the sign Libra on the trump Strength.

But there is an obvious problem. Leo is the sign of the lion, a beast symbolic of virility and strength, and Libra is the sign of the scales, the primary symbol of justice. The trump Strength shows in its picture a lion, and the trump Justice shows in its picture a set of scales. It was obvious to Mathers, and indeed would be obvious to almost anyone, that it would be more appropriate to link the trump Justice with Libra, and the trump Strength with Leo. How could he do this? The Hebrew letters could not be inverted. The associations of the zodiac signs with the Simple letters could not be changed, since they are quite explicit in *Sepher Yetzirah*. The only thing to do was to invert the locations of trumps Justice and Strength, and this Mathers did. He renumbered Justice as XI and placed it after the Wheel of Fortune, and renumbered Strength as VIII and placed it after the Chariot. This corrected the obvious error in symbolism on these two trumps.

Here is the sequence of trumps used by the Golden Dawn, along with their Kabbalistic associations from *Sepher Yetzirah*. The names of some of the trumps were updated by Mathers, based primarily on suggestions in the writings of Court de Gébelin and Éliphas Lévi.

0. Fool—Aleph (Air)
I. Magician—Beth (Mercury)
II. High Priestess—Gimel (Moon)
III. Empress—Daleth (Venus)
IV. Emperor—He (Aries)
V. Hierophant—Vau (Taurus)
VI. Lovers—Zayin (Gemini)
VII. Chariot—Cheth (Cancer)
VIII. Fortitude—Teth (Leo)
IX. Hermit—Yod (Virgo)
X. Wheel of Fortune—Kaph (Jupiter)
XI. Justice—Lamed (Libra)
XII. Hanged Man—Mem (Water)

XIII. Death—Nun (Scorpio)

XIV. Temperance—Samekh (Sagittarius)

XV. Devil—Ayin (Capricorn)

XVI. Blasted Tower—Pe (Mars)

XVII. The Star—Tzaddi (Aquarius)

XVIII. The Moon—Qoph (Pisces)

XIX. The Sun—Resh (Sun)

XX. Judgement—Shin (Fire)

XXI. Universe—Tau (Saturn)

Mathers chose to call the Juggler the Magician. He changed the Female Pope to the High Priestess, and the Pope to the Hierophant. Strength was called by its common alternative, Fortitude. The World became the Universe.

As you can see by examining the Golden Dawn arrangement of the trumps, the zodiac signs that fall on the twelve Simple letters of the Hebrew alphabet are in their natural order beginning with Aries. This is in keeping with the information presented in *Sepher Yetzirah*. The three elements on the Mother letters cannot really be said to have any fixed order, but they also are placed according to *Sepher Yetzirah*. The planets, however, are a different matter. They do have a natural order, and it is not preserved in *Sepher Yetzirah*—indeed, in the Westcott edition of that Kabbalistic book, which was used as a source by Mathers, the way in which they are intended to be placed on the seven Double letters is not explicit, but is open to interpretation.

ORDER OF THE PLANETS IN *SEPHER YETZIRAH*

The text in *Sepher Yetzirah* reads: "So now, behold the Stars of our World, the Planets which are Seven: the Sun, Venus,

Mercury, Moon, Saturn, Jupiter, and Mars."[10] It is obvious that the planets cannot be applied to the Double letters in this order, since that would result in incompatible matches. It would place Mercury on the Empress, for example, and the Moon on the Wheel of Fortune, which would be symbolically incorrect.

Mathers chose to disregard both the order of the planets presented in the text of *Sepher Yetzirah*, and their natural order. The natural order of the planets is based on their apparent rapidity of motion, as viewed from the surface of the Earth. From slowest to fastest, their order is: Saturn, Jupiter, Mars, Sun, Venus, Mercury, Moon. But from fastest to slowest, their reverse order is: Moon, Mercury, Venus, Sun, Mars, Jupiter, Saturn. Mathers adopted neither ordering but created his own for the Double letters and their associated Tarot trumps.

There are hints in *Sepher Yetzirah* as to how the author of that ancient text intended the planets to be applied to the Double letters. He gives sets of opposites for each of the letters, and it is possible to apply these sets to the seven planets, thus generating a list of the planets on the Double letters. Which planet matches which pair of opposite qualities is a matter of conjecture. Here is the relevant text, from the fourth chapter of *Sepher Yetzirah*:

The Seven double letters, Beth, Gimel, Daleth, Kaph, Peh, Resh, and Tau have each two sounds associated with them. They are referred to Life, Peace, Wisdom, Riches, Grace, Fertility, and Power. The two sounds of each letter are the hard and the soft—the aspirated and the softened. They are called Double, because each letter presents a contrast or permutation; thus Life and Death; Peace and War; Wisdom and Folly; Riches and Poverty; Grace and Indignation; Fertility and Solitude; Power and Servitude.[11]

Matching up the qualities of the planets with these pairs of opposites, we might get the following list, which may be how the author of *Sepher Yetzirah* intended the planets to be assigned to the letters.

Beth—Life and Death—Sun
Gimel—Peace and War—Mars
Daleth—Wisdom and Folly—Saturn
Kaph—Riches and Poverty—Mercury
Pe—Grace and Indignation—Venus
Resh—Fertility and Solitude—Moon
Tau—Power and Servitude—Jupiter

This arrangement is only conjecture on my part. In any case, it does not match very well the nature of the Tarot trumps that fall on the seven Double letters of the Hebrew alphabet. It would place the planet Mars on the trump the High Priestess, which seems obviously wrong. Even had Mathers derived this list, he would not have used it.

The key innovations of Mathers and the Golden Dawn with regard to the order of the trumps and their esoteric correspondences are thus the explicit numbering of the Fool as zero, and the placement of the Fool at the head of the trumps; the inversion of the locations and Roman numerals of Justice and Fortitude; and the unique assignment of the planets to the seven Double letters of the Hebrew alphabet.

TRUMP SEQUENCE OF ALEISTER CROWLEY

Aleister Crowley (1875–1947), who was a member of the Golden Dawn and perhaps possessed the greatest esoteric knowledge of the Tarot of any man who has ever lived, made surprisingly few innovations in the order of the trumps. He regarded the Golden Dawn arrangement, which Mathers had received from the Secret Chiefs—they conveyed to him psychically the correct locations of the planets on the Double letters—as received sacred wisdom, and did not attempt on his own initiative to meddle with it. He may have had a low regard for Mathers after departing the Golden Dawn under a black cloud, but he always held the Secret Chiefs in the deepest respect.

It was only when Crowley's guardian angel, Aiwass, came to him while Crowley was visiting Cairo, Egypt, in the year 1904, and dictated to Crowley a holy book titled *Liber AL vel Legis*, or the *Book of the Law*, that Crowley felt bold enough to modify the sequence of the Tarot trumps. In the received text of this book is written the statement, "All these old letters of my Book are aright; but [Tzaddi] is not the Star." [12] The word "Tzaddi" was not written out, but was in the form of the Hebrew letter Tzaddi. The "old letters" obviously refer to the ancient Hebrew alphabet. The reference to "my book" is to the book of Thoth, another name among occultists for the Tarot. The "Star," which is capitalized in Crowley's received text, must refer to the Tarot trump the Star.

In the Golden Dawn arrangement, XVII the Star is linked with the Hebrew letter Tzaddi, and the zodiac sign Aquarius.

The astrological Age of Aquarius is dawning. Crowley identified it with his coming Aeon of Horus, prophesied in the *Book of the Law*, when the Antichrist, son of the Great Beast, would reign supreme. Crowley believed himself to be the Great Beast, so the placement of the trump assigned to the zodiac sign Aquarius naturally held great significance for him.

For years Crowley puzzled about this cryptic message. If Tzaddi was not the Tarot trump the Star, to which trump should it be assigned? The solution reached by Crowley in his book the *Book of Thoth* is based on the inversion of the trumps Justice and Strength made by Mathers in the Golden Dawn Tarot. Crowley drew the twelve signs of the zodiac in their natural order around the rim of a reclining oval, with Pisces on its left side and Virgo on its right side. When this is done, the inversion made by Mathers may be represented graphically by pinching the right end of the oval and giving it a twist to form a little loop, so that the signs of Leo and Libra exchange places around the pivot of Virgo. To balance this change, Crowley took the other end of the oval of the zodiac and gave it a similar twist around the pivot of Pisces to form a second loop, so that the signs Aquarius and Aries changes places. In this way, the model of the zodiac was balanced.[13]

By this trick, Crowley determined to his own satisfaction that Tzaddi was "not the Star" but was, instead, the Emperor. The trump the Star receives Aquarius and the Hebrew letter Tzaddi in the Golden Dawn arrangement, and the trump the Emperor receives Aries and the Hebrew letter He. Crowley inverted this assignment. He did not make this change with the same degree of elegance as Mathers, however. Instead of giving the Emperor the Roman numeral XVII and the Star the Roman numeral IV, Crowley left them where they were in the sequence of the trumps and broke the continuity of the Hebrew alphabet, inverting the two Hebrew letters, along with their linked esoteric correspondences.

This seems inconsistent on Crowley's part. To exactly balance the change made by Mathers in the loop at the other end of the zodiac, Crowley should have exchanged the Roman numerals and the placements of the trumps the Emperor and the Star, but kept the integrity of the sequence of the Hebrew alphabet, which has been established for thousands of years. Mathers moved the trumps—he did not move the Hebrew letters. Crowley should have done the same, had he wished to mirror the change made by Mathers.

Instead, Crowley chose to return the Roman numeral VIII to Justice, and XI to Strength, which places them back in their original locations in the Marseilles sequence of the trumps, but he retained the Hebrew letters and zodiac signs given to these trumps by Mathers, thereby violating the sequence of the Hebrew alphabet a second time.

In the Tarot trumps of Crowley's Thoth deck, the card of the Emperor bears the Hebrew letter Tzaddi, but still retains the zodiac sign Aries. Similarly, the card of the Star bears the Hebrew letter He, but retains the zodiac sign Aquarius. This appears to be an error, since it would be assumed that the zodiac signs should have been changed along with the Hebrew letters—indeed, this was done in the table of the trumps that appears near the end of Crowley's *Book of Thoth*.[14] Below is Crowley's arrangement of the Tarot trumps, as it appears in that table. He has changed many of the names of the trumps, but not so radically that they cannot be recognized. Justice was called Adjustment, Strength became Lust, and Temperance was called by Crowley Art.

0. Fool—Aleph (Air)
I. Magus—Beth (Mercury)
II. Priestess—Gimel (Moon)
III. Empress—Daleth (Venus)
IV. Emperor—Tzaddi (Aquarius)
V. Hierophant—Vau (Taurus)
VI. Lovers—Zayin (Gemini)
VII. Chariot—Cheth (Cancer)
VIII. Adjustment—Lamed (Libra)
IX. Hermit—Yod (Virgo)
X. Fortune—Kaph (Jupiter)
XI. Lust—Teth (Leo)
XII. Hanged Man—Mem (Water)
XIII. Death—Nun (Scorpio)
XIV. Art—Samekh (Sagittarius)
XV. Devil—Ayin (Capricorn)
XVI. Tower—Pe (Mars)
XVII. The Star—He (Aries)
XVIII. The Moon—Qoph (Pisces)
XIX. The Sun—Resh (Sun)
XX. Judgment—Shin (Fire)
XXI. Universe—Tau (Saturn)

TRUMP SEQUENCE OF DONALD TYSON

The Tarot has been central to my esoteric studies and practices for almost forty years. I have spent considerable time thinking about the arrangement of the trumps, and have come to some conclusions that I wish to offer here, for those who may be interested in my own sequence and occult correspondences for the trumps. This material previously appeared in the appendix to my book *Portable Magic* (Llewellyn Worldwide, 2006), which deals with the use of the Tarot for works of ritual magic. Since I believe it is important, I wish to make it as widely available as possible.

My own sense is that Crowley's change is not valid. It does apply a kind of balance to the loop of the zodiac, and Crowley was obsessed with balance in magic—he believed that all true magicians have an innate sense of harmony and balance, and that they naturally abhor anything in their art that is lacking in symmetry. Well, maybe so, but I see no necessity to balance the inversion of Justice and Strength made by Mathers. The change has its own inherent balance, in that each trump replaces the other. I believe that the change made by Mathers is valid, and indeed inevitable, given the symbolism on the two cards and the zodiac signs involved. Leo must go with Strength, and Virgo must go with Justice.

My primary problem with the Golden Dawn sequence of the trumps lies in the Double letters of the Hebrew alphabet, which are linked with the seven planets. In astrology and in magic, the planets have a very definite ordering, as I explained above. Since the zodiac signs are arranged on the twelve Simple letters in their natural order, it seems to me that it would make good sense to arrange the planets on the seven Double letters in their natural order as well. The reason Mathers did not do this is because it creates some problems. However, in my opinion these issues are not beyond solution, even though some of the changes I propose may seem fairly radical.

The placements of Mercury on the trump of the Magician by Mathers, through the mediation of the Double letter Beth, and the Moon on the High Priestess through the mediation of the Double letter Gimel, have a rightness that would be difficult to challenge. This suggests that if the planets are placed on the trumps in their natural astrological order, it will be an ascending order from quickest and nearest, to slowest and furthest removed. But there is a serious problem. The first planet in this ascending order is the Moon, not Mercury, which is the second planet. To simply apply the planets to the trumps of the Double letters would result in the Magician receiving the Moon, and the High Priestess receiving Mercury. This does not seem symbolically correct.

The solution is obvious, but daring—to invert the location and Roman numerals of trumps the Magician and the High Priestess, so that the High Priestess receives the Roman numeral I and is placed directly after the Fool, and the Magician receives the Roman numeral II and comes after the High Priestess. It is safe to say that this change is the most likely to arouse controversy among those I have advocated. There is a traditional prejudice that the male Magician should come before the female Priestess. However, when we consider why this should be so, it is not easy to come up with a reason. There is something to be said for the Priestess opening the sequence of the trumps—for the Fool, although he is nominally placed at the beginning, really has no place of his own, as his zero designation indicates, but moves where he wills, and relates to all the other trumps equally.

The pillars of the Priestess on modern versions of the trump are like an open doorway ushering the neophyte into the mysteries of the Tarot. They would seem to indicate a natural numbering for this trump of II. It should be understood, however, that the pillars derive from the numbering of this trump with the Roman numeral II in the Marseilles deck. The pillars are not a part of the oldest Tarot designs, where the trumps had no numbering, and no single set sequence. It might be argued that the pillars were suggested by the back of the chair in which La Papesse sits in the Marseilles deck, or by the scrolling at the ends of the veil behind her head, but the posts of the chair back are not pillars, nor are the scrolls of the veil. The pillars are a relatively modern esoteric interpretation—they were described by Lévi, and his description was highly influential on later Tarot designers, but they do not appear in the trump design of de Gébelin.

There is another change necessary to apply the planets in their natural ascending order on the seven Double letters of the Hebrew alphabet and their corresponding trumps. In the Golden Dawn arrangement, Jupiter is placed on trump X the Wheel, and the planet the Sun is placed on trump XIX the Sun. I asked myself, if the planet the Moon is not located on trump XVIII the Moon in the Golden Dawn arrangement, why should it be necessary to locate the planet the Sun on the trump of the same name? It is not necessary, and indeed not even desirable to do so. When the planets are applied to the trumps of the Double letters in their natural order, it is the Sun that falls on the Wheel, and Jupiter that falls on the trump the Sun.

This change works very well. The Sun is a great fiery wheel rolling across the heavens and has been characterized in this way in stone age petroglyphs of shamans, and in numerous systems of mythology around the world. It is symbolically apt to link the astrological planet the Sun with the trump the Wheel of Fortune. As for the trump of the Sun—what could be more appropriate to represent it than the beaming countenance of the god Jupiter, as represented by his planet? Jupiter is the dispenser of benevolent laws, the patriarch of the heavens. The planets Jupiter and the Sun have always had harmonious natures in astrology.

It can be seen that by inverting the locations of the trumps the Magician and the High Priestess, all seven of the planets fall on highly appropriate trumps when applied to the sequence of the Double letters in their natural ascending order. The placement of the planet the Sun on the Wheel of Fortune is so right, it is difficult to imagine how Mathers could have avoided making it. Perhaps the designation of Jupiter as the "greater fortune" in astrology swayed his judgment. Even so, I cannot agree with his choice, and believe that the Sun should be on the Wheel, and Jupiter on the trump the Sun.

There are actually three fortunes in astrology, as Cornelius Agrippa pointed out in his *Occult Philosophy*: "There are three Fortunes amongst the planets."[15] These are the Sun, Jupiter, and Venus. However, Jupiter is usually called the Greater Fortune and Venus the Lesser Fortune. I mention this merely to point out that the Sun has at least as much connection with the Wheel of Fortune, thematically, as Jupiter. Both Sun and Jupiter are astrological fortunes. It also shows the close tie between the planet Jupiter and the trump the Sun.

There is one more essential change in the sequence of the trumps that must be made before they can be consid-

ered perfected. It involves the inversion of trumps XIV
Temperance and VII the Chariot. It has long been my conviction that the zodiac sign Cancer does not belong with
the Chariot. In spite of the valiant attempts by Mathers
and other occultists to justify its location on the Chariot, there is nothing warlike about the sign of Cancer. The
characterization of the fierce Crab with her savage pin-
cers raised for battle strikes me with amusement every
time I encounter it. The sign of the Crab is not fierce—it is
watery and feminine.

Similarly, I found nothing appropriate in linking the
rather warlike zodiac sign of the Archer, Sagittarius, with
the feminine and watery trump Temperance. Indeed, there
seems no obvious symbolic harmony between the two. The
bow and arrow is a weapon of war and a weapon of the
hunt. It is designed to deal death. But the waters poured
between the two vessels on the trump Temperance are the
waters of life.

I have no hesitation in advocating that these trumps
be inverted, and their Roman numerals exchanged, so that
Temperance is placed just after the Lovers, and receives the
number VII, and the Chariot is placed just after Death, and
receives the number XIV. Indeed, this change strikes me as
the most obvious and inevitable of all the changes that I
have made, and I am amazed that Mathers did not make it
himself.

You will notice that this results in a series of violent or warlike cards: the Hanged Man, Death, the Chariot, the Devil, and
the Tower. In the common sequence of the trumps, and the
Golden Dawn sequence as well, the card Temperance breaks
up this set. Equally, the older placement of the Chariot seems

completely wrong—it comes in the midst of a peaceful series of trumps, after the Hierophant and the Lovers, and before Strength and the Hermit. Strength, sometimes titled Fortitude, is not violent, but is the strength of self-control and restraint. The overtly violent and warlike Chariot is completely wrong for this series.

Here, then, is my rectified sequence of the Tarot trumps, according to my best judgment. It is my experience that it lends itself very well to the paths on the Tree of Life—better than the Golden Dawn sequence. Of course those accustomed to using the Golden Dawn arrangement on the Tree will find it an effort to change mental gears and try something new, but those who make the change will not want to go back.

0. Fool—Aleph (Air)
I. High Priestess—Beth (Moon)
II. Magician—Gimel (Mercury)
III. Empress—Daleth (Venus)
IV. Emperor—He (Aries)
V. Hierophant—Vau (Taurus)
VI. Lovers—Zayin (Gemini)
VII. Temperance—Cheth (Cancer)
VIII. Strength—Teth (Leo)
IX. Hermit—Yod (Virgo)
X. Wheel—Kaph (Sun)
XI. Justice—Lamed (Libra)
XII. Hanged Man—Mem (Water)
XIII. Death—Nun (Scorpio)
XIV. Chariot—Samekh (Sagittarius)
XV. Devil—Ayin (Capricorn)

XVI. Tower—Pe (Mars)
XVII. The Star—Tzaddi (Aquarius)
XVIII. The Moon—Qoph (Pisces)
XIX. The Sun—Resh (Jupiter)
XX. Judgement—Shin (Fire)
XXI. World—Tau (Saturn)

NOTES

1. Decker, Depaulis, and Dummett, p. 25.

2. Ibid., p. 41.

3. Ibid., p. 43.

4. Ibid., p. 62.

5. Ibid., p. 70.

6. Lévi, p. 386.

7. Christian, p. 110.

8. Papus, p. 184.

9. Waite, *Pictorial Key*, p. 29.

10. Westcott, p. 23.

11. Ibid., p. 22.

12. Crowley, *Book of the Law*, p. 26.

13. Crowley, *Book of Thoth*, pp. 9–11.

14. Ibid., p. 278.

15. Agrippa, p. 250.

10

Time and Magic

We tend to think of time as a linear sequence of events that moves in one direction. It is a flowing river down which the boats of our souls are swept with their bows pointing backward. Or we march blindly along the road of life, our footsteps moving to the rhythmic swing of a clock pendulum, our heartbeat the ticking of its mechanism. Or we fall helplessly, unable to catch ourselves until the final impact of death.

In exoteric Eastern philosophies, where time is perceived to be rhythmic, circular, or spiral, it is nonetheless usually described as an orderly and unvarying sequence of moments. Karma is founded on this underlying assumption. Effect follows cause. The experiences in past lives influence the condition of our future incarnations.

There is another, quite different view of the nature of time, a shamanic view in which time is not seen as a series of moments arrayed like beads on a string but as an indivisible whole, all points of which are equally accessible. In this magical awareness, time is not a wave that we ride with our faces forever turned backwards. Our nominal consciousness is the wave, and time is a dimension of the cosmic sea of mind. When we look with the "I" consciousness, we ride the wave; when we look with the "All" consciousness, we become the sea.

Eastern mystics have found it impossible to adequately convey the condition of *samadhi*, but a study of their descriptions shows that during the highest states of meditation, space and time merge and past and future become equally accessible in the timeless nowhere of the infinite present. Attempts to describe the ultimate mystical ecstasy show an astounding uniformity of content even though they span all cultures and all ages of the human race. They prove it is possible for the human mind to transcend the arbitrary barriers of time imposed upon the fabric of the universe by our limited everyday consciousness.

If we accept as a working hypothesis that under certain unusual conditions the human mind can go beyond its rigid perception of time as a linear sequence and thus free itself from the tyranny of the present moment, we gain a novel and potentially useful way of looking at magical and paranormal events.

Under this model, divination can be explained as the awareness of the diviner casting forward or backward through the dimension of time in search of significant events. Mechanical aids, such as the Tarot, runes, crystals, and so on, are seen to be useful only insofar as they promote the induction of an altered consciousness allowing this time-casting. A similar explanation covers prophecy.

The extremely common occurrence of déjà vu, the sense of having had a certain experience in the past, becomes explicable as the sudden involuntary recollection of a future memory—in other words, in déjà vu the mind goes forward and recalls a memory of the actual present moment. From the restricted framework of everyday awareness, this future memory of the present is interpreted as a past memory, the only form of memory we accept.

Precognition involves nothing more mysterious than a fleeting awareness of a future event that we either are going to experience ourselves or are going to learn about via others. Such an awareness of the event must exist somewhere in our future consciousness, or we would never know that we had experienced precognition in the first place. A sense of impending personal danger—the most frequent type of pre-cognitive event—would only indicate that the mind had for a brief time ceased to be aware of the present moment and had instead become aware of a highly significant future moment.

Ritual magicians know that the purpose of a ritual may sometimes be achieved immediately following its working even though the mechanics of its fulfillment have taken days or weeks. Aleister Crowley observed this curious time anomaly: "I have noticed that the effect of a Magical Work has followed it so closely that it must have been started before the time of the Work. E.g. I work to-night to make X in Paris write to me. I get the letter the next morning, so that it must have been written before the Work."[1] In such cases it may be that the magician unconsciously casts his mind forward to the fulfillment of his desire and then schedules his ritual to coincide with that event.

The full implications of this magical awareness of the wholeness of time are staggering in scope. If all moments of time exist equally in some vast eternal now, then nothing is ever lost. The great works of literature and philosophy, and even the most ancient achievements in painting, sculpture, and architecture, are not irretrievably forgotten but accessible to a mind that can transcend the present and then selectively recall a specific moment of the past.

This is the essential understanding behind the magical notion of the akashic records popularized by Madame Blavatsky, the founder of Theosophy. The entire history of the human race is forever fixed in the *akasha*, a subtle ether underlying all things, like a fly trapped in a tear of amber. It is an immensely positive and exciting view. All history, and indeed all the mysteries of the future, potentially lie scattered at our feet, waiting only for us to gather them up.

This holistic view of time might be used to justify past-life regression, which seems so indefensible when subjected to the rigid criteria of physical science. It would not necessarily mean that those who regress remember their own lives, but it would provide one explanation as to how they might remember the lives of actual historical persons, as opposed to merely fantasizing about fictional characters.

By transcending the present moment and the linear concept of time, a living person could get into contact and converse with one of the great minds of the past, a Socrates or a Michelangelo or a Shakespeare. To such a person living in the past, the communication would appear to come from a disembodied voice heard in the head, or from a projected externalized spirit. Interestingly enough, the Greek philosopher Socrates had a personal daemon who advised him and warned him of impending dangers by means of various signs. Extending this idea, the spirits perceived by modern channelers may actually be the time-tripping minds of human beings, or inhuman intelligences, who are living elsewhere in our time ocean.

Metaphysically, this magical concept of time means that we never cease to be, but exist eternally as a part of the fabric of the universe, perhaps to be played and replayed over and over by some higher consciousness in the same way the recording of a song exists on a disc or a story exists in a book, to be experienced whenever desired. If true, no good deed is ever really forgotten or unappreciated. By the same token, no evil act ever escapes notice, not even when it is done alone and in darkness.

Mystics have succeeded in transcending the present moment to achieve a timeless and placeless awareness of being. The ways to attain this transcendence are extremely difficult but are well known and documented. However, such mystical awareness is not directed to any specific event in time. Quite the opposite; mystics strenuously avoid descending into particular awareness of individual visions, voices, or beings because they regard such particularization as a distraction from the highest and purest state of mind.

It remains the challenge of those experimenting with the paranormal and the occult to develop procedural techniques that will shatter their restrictive linear, unidirectional concept of time, and yet still allow them to retain their desire to sample and retrieve particular moments in the past or future. Such conscious and deliberate time-tripping, if it ever becomes possible, will be the ultimate human adventure.

NOTES

1. Crowley, *Magick*, pp. 74–75.

11

The Fairy Godmother

A recurring figure in the popular folklore of northern Europe is the fairy godmother. This mysterious woman appears by magic to attend the birth or christening of an infant, often a child who is seemingly of no special importance. She may be alone or accompanied by other women. She comes uninvited either to bless or curse the child, displays various magical abilities, and then just as mysteriously departs, perhaps to reappear at some distant future date, or perhaps never to be seen again. This quaint figure of children's fairy tales has more importance in the history of Western magic than most people realize. Let us take a look at some of her folk characteristics, and then consider her true identity and significance in the context of the Western esoteric tradition.

The first thing that must be observed about fairy godmothers is that they are not nearly so common in ancient folklore as their more modern popularity might cause us to suppose. They appear in two of the most beloved fairy stories—"Sleeping Beauty" and "Cinderella"—both of which were turned into animated films by the Disney Studios. This cinematic treatment helped spread the fable of the fairy godmother far and wide in the 20th century.

SLEEPING BEAUTY

In the story of "Sleeping Beauty" the fairy godmother first appears in the version by Charles Perrault (1628–1703), published in 1697 in France in his hugely popular book *Contes de ma Mère l'Oye* (*Tales of Mother Goose*). In the portion of the tale that concerns us, seven fairies are invited to the christening of a newborn princess by her loving parents, in the hope that they will confer magical gifts upon the child and act as her godmothers. To honor them, the king orders seven plates of gold to be made for them to use at the christening feast. However, an eighth fairy who is older and unattractive decides to come to the christening, and when she sees that no gold plate has been made for her, she feels that her dignity has been slighted.

Six of the fairy godmothers bless the infant girl with various life gifts. The crone is the seventh to approach the child, and she curses the baby with the curse that when she touches a spindle, she will prick her finger and immediately fall dead. One of the fairies who earlier observed the crone has hung back to go last, and although she cannot undo the curse of the evil fairy, she renders it less severe, proclaiming that the girl will not drop dead but will fall asleep for one hundred years, whereupon she will be awakened by the kiss of a prince.

Perrault's version was based on an older story by the Italian Giambattista Basile (*c.* 1566–1632), published posthumously by his sister in 1634 under the title "Sol, Luna e Talia" ("Sun, Moon and Talia"), in which there is no fairy god-mother. In this earlier tale, the name of the baby princess is Talia. At her birth, astrologers cast her horoscope and predict that she will come to harm from a tiny splinter of flax. Her father, the king, takes every precaution to keep her away from flax, but one day the girl sees an old woman spinning flax on a spindle, and out of curiosity decides to try it. A splin-ter of flax gets embedded beneath her fingernail, and she falls down in what appears to be death. The king cannot bring himself to bury his beautiful and beloved child, so he lays her safely to rest on one of his country estates.

After some time has passed, another king who is hunt-ing in the forest comes upon the girl and is so enamored with her apparently lifeless form that he has sex with her, then goes away. Still deep asleep, the girl gives birth to twins, a boy and a girl who are named Sun and Moon. One day, when the boy is unable to find the breast of his uncon-scious mother to suckle, his pangs of hunger cause him to suckle her finger, and he draws out the splinter of flax. She immediately awakens.

The earliest version of the story, "Perceforest," published in France in 1528, has goddesses in place of fairy godmoth-ers. In this version, three goddesses visit a female child named Zellandine at her birth celebration. They are obvi-ously intended to bring to mind the three Fates of Greek mythology, although their names are different. The first, Lucinda, confers the gift of health on the infant, but the second goddess, Themis, curses the child because the god-dess took the absence of a knife beside her plate at the feast as a personal slight. Her curse is that Zellandine will one day impale her finger on the point of a distaff, and sleep until it is removed. The third goddess, Venus, cannot undo the curse placed on the head of the baby but mitigates it by prophesying that one day the distaff will be removed and the curse lifted.

In the popular version of "Sleeping Beauty" recorded by the Brothers Grimm, titled "Briar Rose" and published in 1812, the fairy godmothers number thirteen, twelve who give gifts to the infant princess and one who curses the child out of spite. The gift of the final good fairy softens the curse of the twelfth. Much was made of this number of fairy godmothers, but since they were only eight in number in Perrault's older version of the story, the importance of the number thirteen may have been exaggerated.

CINDERELLA

The story of "Cinderella" goes back as far as the ancient Greek historian Strabo (64 BC—*c.* 24 AD), who wrote in his *Geographica* about an Egyptian girl named Rhodopis who was forced to wash clothes in a stream while the other servants attended a celebration sponsored by the Pharaoh, Amasis. While she was working, an eagle snatched away her rose-gilded sandal and carried it to Memphis, then dropped it at the feet of Amasis. The Pharaoh was enraptured by the fineness and smallness of the sandal and asked all the women of Egypt to try it on, so that he could locate its owner. When Rhodopis was able to put on the sandal, Amasis married her and made her his queen.

Nothing here about a fairy godmother. This magical figure does not appear in the "Cinderella" story until the 1697 version of Charles Perrault. In his tale, a widower takes in

marriage a proud and cruel woman with two grown daughters. His meek and modest daughter by his first marriage is
forced by her stepmother to do all the housework, which
she performs without complaint. It is her habit to sit amid
the cinders, hence her name Cinderella (Cendrillon, in
French). One day the prince of the land decides to host a
ball for the purpose of choosing a wife. The stepsisters go,
but Cinderella has no dress that is suitable for so grand an
occasion.

As she weeps in sorrow, her fairy godmother appears,
and tells the girl that she will be attending the ball after
all. The fairy turns a pumpkin into a coach, mice into its
team of horses, a rat into the coachman, and lizards into
footmen. She creates for Cinderella a gown and a pair of
glass slippers, but warns the girl to be home before midnight, since that is when the spell will be broken. Everything goes well and Cinderella is the belle of the ball, but
the next night when a second ball is held, she becomes care-
less of time and departs in haste just before midnight, leaving behind her one of her glass slippers. The prince searches
the kingdom, seeking the girl whose foot fits the slipper.
When Cinderella tries on the shoe, he knows he has found
her, and this is confirmed when she brings forth the other
glass slipper, which has not vanished away along with the
coach and her gown.

In the version of "Cinderella" ("Aschenputtel" in German) published in 1812 by the Brothers Grimm, there is no
fairy godmother. Instead, Cinderella is helped by the ghost
of her dead mother, represented by a pair of birds that
perch in a tree growing above her mother's grave. Thus the

supernatural element is still present, but it is ancestral spirit in nature rather than fairy.

ROLE OF THE FAIRY GODMOTHER

These examples should be sufficient to give some notion of the stereotypical role of the fairy godmother in fairy tales, particular the literary tales written by French writers in the 17th and 18th centuries, such as Marie-Catherine d'Aulnoy (1650–1705). These were not true folk tales but imitations of folk tales, or composed stories based in part on genuine folk tales. In these stories the fairy godmother makes more frequent appearances than she does in true folk tales.

It is the usual role of a human godmother to give a christening gift, and to watch over the spiritual education of the child. The fairy godmother takes on the same obligations as a mortal godmother, though the reason these obligations are assumed is not always clear. Sometimes it is done as a fair exchange, as when the seven fairies were invited to the feast by the king and given golden plates as gifts; other times, it seems motivated by some unseen occult requirement. The child is destined from birth by the Fates to receive the gift of its fairy godmother, who is merely an instrument of destiny. Indeed, the Fates of Greek mythology are probably the prototypes of the fairy godmothers of later children's fiction, as suggested by their thinly veiled appearance in the 1528 French version of "Sleeping Beauty" described earlier.

In mythology, the gifts of the gods can be both a blessing and a curse, depending on the circumstances under which they are received and the uses to which they are put. Fairy tales simplify this dichotomy by making the gifts of good fairies always good, and the gifts of evil fairies always evil. In life, what seems good may prove to be a curse, and what seems a burden may in the end be revealed as a blessing. Even in fairy tales, good may come of evil, and the curse of the evil fairy godmother results in great happiness in the end, when all problems have been resolved.

An important factor to consider about the role of a godmother is her accepted obligation to watch over the spiritual development and well-being of the child. In Christianity this often takes the symbolic form of the gift of a new Bible to the baby. Spirituality is broader than any particular religion, and if we consider the obligation of the godmother in these terms, she is charged with the general spiritual health of the child. In fairy tales this is symbolized by the various physical and moral virtues that are given to the child as gifts, such as beauty and wisdom.

NATURE OF THE FAIRY GODMOTHER

The fairy godmother is a spirit, not a being of flesh and blood. This is seldom made clear in the fairy tales, where she is given a physical body and is made to dine at the christening feast. In ancient folklore and mythology, spiritual beings often receive physical bodies. For example, the angels in the Old Testament are described as being like men in every respect. They eat, drink, sleep, and have material bodies. Similarly, the witch's familiar is usually described in physical terms, and malicious spirits such as incubi and vampires are credited with physical forms.

The archetype of the evil fairy godmother is Grandmother Lilith, a female demon of the ancient Sumerians and Babylonians who made her way into Hebrew folklore via the Babylonian Captivity of the 6th century BC, during which the Judeans were taken as slaves from the Kingdom of Judah to Babylonia. During their stay in Babylonia, they picked up much of the mythology of the Babylonians, including the myth of Lilith, who was fabled to be a horrible old crone with unkempt, long gray hair and long dirty fingernails, yellowed teeth, and glaring red eyes, who visited the cribs of newborn infants. Sometimes Lilith merely played with the infant, but at other times, seemingly on a capricious inclination, she would kill the baby by stealing away its breath.

Lilith is not often regarded as a fairy. She is more likely to be classed among the demons of hell, but this is an arbitrary classification, since she is Sumerian in origin and predates the Christian concept of hell, with its orderly demonic hierarchies.

Fairies are indigenous to Celtic lands, although similar nature spirits exist around the world. Perhaps more than any other spirit, they are apt to be regarded as physical by those who believe in them. They live in a kind of parallel universe that has portals into our reality under certain hills recognized as fairy mounds. The doorways to these fairy realms materialize from nowhere to allow the fairies to enter or leave, and just as swiftly vanish, leaving no trace. This transition from the fairy realm to the human realm happens most often at twilight, in the gloaming when the world is caught in a timeless moment between day and night. They are also more frequent at the equinoxes, when the seasons are in balance.

Transitional periods of the day or year facilitate the transition between fairy reality and human reality. A portal of any kind is a transition between one place and another. In the gloaming, fairies become visible to the eyes of those psychic enough to see them, but at other times of the day they are more difficult to see, unless they wish to be seen. The birth of an infant is a kind of life transition, from the spiritual reality into the physical reality, so it is natural that fairies would appear at this time.

It is a mystery as to why fairies should wish to associate with humanity, yet this has always been the case throughout their history. They are known to appear to men, women, and children, and to abduct them into their fairy realm, where they may keep them forever, or may release them after a prolonged time has passed. The fairy practice of kidnapping children, and leaving a fairy child in their place, is frequently mentioned in the literature about these strange and somewhat frightening spirits.

As usual, these events are described as completely material in the accounts of them that have come down to us, but it is more probable that they are spiritual events. A man is not physically taken to fairyland; he falls into a trance or coma, and is taken there on an astral level of reality. There are records of those who, when they lay down and went to sleep on fairy mounds, fell into a coma or even died. I say that it is "probable" that these are merely spiritual events, not certain, because accounts exist of those who simply disappeared for days or years, and who when they suddenly reappeared, told tales of having lived among the fairies in their world.

The parallels with alien abductions are obvious. But whether these parallels suggest that aliens are fairies, or that fairies are aliens, or that both are something else that has yet to be accurately described, I leave to your conjecture. It seems fairly certain that there is a some underlying connection between fairy abductions and alien abductions.

Can the fairy godmother of folklore be an alien being who confers upon a newborn child certain superhuman abilities? Is this the root of this persistent motif? Children abducted by aliens are sometimes said to be altered or enhanced in various ways—to possess psychic abilities that they did not have before the abduction. There is also the belief that aliens are breeding a race of hybrid children, half human and half alien, who possess more than human abilities. Again, this has parallels in the ancient belief that spirits could interbreed with human women and engender offspring. Jesus is one such being, according to this view— half human and half something else.

TUTELARY SPIRITS

A tutelary spirit is a spirit that teaches, guides, and protects a human being. The idea that certain spirits watch over and protect human beings with whom they are in some way linked is universal. This belief has taken many forms, as different human cultures try to come to terms with it. Often it is looked upon as protection by dead ancestors of their descendants. Whole religions exist based on this belief, that the dead watch over their children and children's children. It is a reasonable explanation as to why a spiritual being would bother to protect a living person, or even take an interest in that individual.

Sometimes, spirits associated with certain places develop links with the people who live there, and come to watch over and guide them. For example, a nature spirit dwelling in a spring might form an attachment to a man who owned the land occupied by the spring; or a house spirit might become fond of a person living in the same house. A fairy associated with a certain thorn bush in a farmer's field could form some sort of personal interaction with the farmer—although in the case of fairies, that interaction is just as likely to be harmful as helpful. But fairies are capable of affection, and even love, for human beings. Their affection is capricious, and easily turns into jealousy or malice.

The ancient Greeks believed that certain special men, who were by their nature semi-divine, had daemons—tutelary spirits—joined to their lives. The most famous man who was guided by such a daemon was the philosopher Socrates, whose daemon was well known to his contemporaries.[1] Socrates made no secret of the fact that his tutelary spirit often intervened in his life when he was about to make a mistake, to warn him not to do it. The day Socrates drank the hemlock brew that killed him, he told his friends that he knew it was the right thing to do, because his spirit had not warned him against drinking it.

Some men were even believed to be favored by the gods. Often they were hybrids, half mortal and half divine by nature. The god who was one parent of such a person would continue to watch over him throughout life. These demigods were the heroes of ancient Greek mythology, such as Hercules and Achilles. The belief that one of their parents was divine was just a way of trying to explain why they were favored by spirits in their lives. Some Greek writers held the view that Socrates was semi-divine, as were Aristotle and Alexander the Great, just because of the great works they accomplished during their lifetimes, which seemed to their biographers to be beyond unaided human abilities. A human being capable of miraculous works must have superhuman aid—such was the common opinion among the Greeks.

A more plebian notion arose among the Greeks that every man received at birth both a good daemon and an evil daemon. These two tutelary spirits were at constant war with each other, which cancelled out most of their effects on the life of the person to whom they were attached. The good daemon whispered sound and helpful advice, while the evil daemon suggested actions that were worthless or harmful. This idea carried over into Christianity in the form of the good angel that is supposed to sit on the right shoulder of every person, and the evil angel that sits on the left shoulder.

The good daemon and evil daemon take the forms in the fairy tales of the good fairy godmother and the evil fairy godmother, whose efforts to some extent cancel each other out. The good daemon cannot simply banish the evil daemon, but it can to some degree moderate the mischief the evil daemon is able to cause.

FAMILIAR SPIRITS

Most people recognize the term *familiar* in connection with witches, who were supposed by the demonologists of the Inquisition during the Renaissance to have demons (evil spirits) that served their needs and desires. However, the concept of familiar spirits is much broader than that. A familiar is any spirit that is attached to a human being.

Familiars perform various functions. They teach, guide, protect, and also serve. Some were considered to be low spirits, in the nature of servants, while others are looked upon as more sophisticated and powerful. The Church regarded all familiars as subservient demons, who pretended to serve the witch while really working to corrupt the witch's soul. This is a narrow and simplistic view, dictated by the religious dogma of those who held it. However, familiars do appear to be of varying degrees of power and sophistication. Some are simple beings that fulfill well-defined and limited functions. Others are complex and act more as partners in the lives of those human beings to whom they are linked.

Shamans would sometimes take to wife familiar spirits who were, in many respects, their superiors in both power and wisdom. They would also have mortal wives upon whom they engendered children. It would not be unreasonable to assume that the spirit wife of a shaman would confer various benefits and gifts on the head of the newborn child of the shaman by his mortal wife.

Some spirits are associated with entire bloodlines. The best known is the water spirit Melusina, one of the *dames blanches* (white ladies) who watched over the descendants of Raymond of Poitou. The white ladies were considered to be fairies. Raymond married Melusina and had children by her. Even after Melusina abandoned him because he broke his vow to her that he should never look upon her on a Saturday, she continued to watch over their descendants, and would appear wailing with sorrow when some great catastrophe was about to befall the bloodline.

Conclusion

So what exactly is a fairy godmother? She is a spiritual being who either blesses or curses the life of a newborn child. Because she is a spirit with the power of working magic, her blessing or curse has practical consequences. The curse of one spirit may be countered, at least in part, by the blessing of another spirit. These spirits are linked with the lives of the infants they visit, but the exact nature of that connection remains unclear. It may be based on a blood relationship. The infants may be spirit-human hybrids or descendants of such hybrids; or it may be that the fairy godmother is a dead ancestor of the infant and is not really a fairy at all.

Most people will dismiss the whole notion of fairy godmothers as absurd. However, it is undeniable that some human beings appear to be born with gifts and abilities that are so far above those of humanity in general that they are looked upon as supernatural. The myth of the fairy godmother is one attempt to explain where such extraordinary gifts come from. It is somewhat simplistic, as are most mythic explanations, but like most myths, it has a seed of truth at its heart that is worth considering.

Notes

1. Beaumont, pp. 21–23.

12

Black Magic

This article examines the subject of black magic. Before beginning, it seems necessary to make the observation that to talk about a thing is not the same as advocating that thing. It should not be needful to say this, but many persons seem to assume that the discussion of any topic is a kind of advocacy. For the benefit of those individuals: even though I am writing about black magic, that does not mean I want you to go out and practice it.

Black magic is a subset of magic in general and involves magic done with malicious intent, which sometimes uses forbidden materials or involves criminal actions. For example, to ritually wish death on an innocent child is an act of black magic, no matter how it is done; but by some definitions, even a praiseworthy purpose may involve black magic if it requires forbidden methods, such as grave robbery to obtain the parts of corpses. Necromancy, which is the magic of the dead, is usually considered to be black magic since it is associated with corpses and things of the dead.

THE *MALLEUS MALEFICARUM*

The opposite of black magic is white magic. You do not encounter references to white magic in the older literature of the Christian demonologists, such as the *Malleus Maleficarum* (1486), because all magic was held to be black by the Church. To the old authorities black magic, when recognized at all, was simply more evil than magic in general. Black magic was called by the Latin term *malefica*, which signifies evil magic. In English, a "malefice" was an evil enchantment, and to "maleficiate" was to bewitch.

The unenlightened authors of the *Malleus Maleficarum*, Heinrich Kramer and James Sprenger, wrote: "Moreover, witchcraft differs from all other harmful and mysterious arts in this point, that of all superstition it is essentially the vilest, the most evil and the worst, wherefore it derives its name from doing evil, and from blaspheming the true faith."[1] By "witchcraft" they intended all forms of magic that they interpreted as coming from the Devil or his demons, including such seemingly benign practices as divination.

Their definition of a witch was anyone who induced evil spirits to perform unnatural wonders. They wrote that "certain angels fell from heaven and are now devils, and we are bound to acknowledge that by their very nature they can do many wonderful things which we cannot do. And those who try to induce others [that is, these devils] to perform such evil wonders are called witches."[2]

During the Renaissance, European witches were frequently accused of black magic by their persecutors, as a way of damning them more completely. In the eyes of the Church, the mere practice of magic in any form was damnable, but deliberately malicious and harmful magic was all the more to be condemned. Witches were said to cause storms at sea and on land, to blight crops, to sicken cattle and other farm beasts, to bewitch their neighbors, and in general to work all manner of mischiefs at the behest of their supposed master, the Devil.

The poor and illiterate country people of the time sought wise women for charms of healing and other useful purposes, but these good works of magic were not recognized by the Church. The universal view of priests and monks was that witches were the slaves of the Devil and that wizards or necromancers bargained with Satan as partners in evil, or even directed his minions for their own private purposes.

Daemonologie

King James the First of England, while he was King James the Sixth of Scotland and still awaiting his ascension to the English throne, wrote a tract about witchcraft titled *Daemonologie* (1597), in which he stated this distinction between witches and magicians: "Surelie, the difference vulgare put betwixt them, is verrie merrie, and in a maner true; for they say, that the Witches ar servantes onelie, and slaues of the Devil; but the Necromanciers are his maisters and commanders."[3]

Of course this view had nothing at all to do with what real magic was all about. The Devil did not play a large part in the magic of either witches or wizards during the 16th century. Magicians were concerned mainly with summoning and commanding spirits for various purposes, and witches spent most of their time healing the sick, predicting the future, making love charms, and banishing the evil eye. Magic is a tool. As is true of any tool, such as a knife, it may be used for works of good or works of evil. No doubt there were genuinely evil witches, but there were many more numerous good witches who were swept up in the witch persecutions and burned or hanged.

CORNELIUS AGRIPPA

Forward-looking thinkers such as Cornelius Agrippa (1486–1535) took a stance exactly opposite that of the demonologists, and held that magic was inherently a noble and worthwhile pursuit. He observed in his *Three Books of Occult Philosophy*, which were written in 1509–10 and circulated in manuscript, but were only published in their entirety in 1533: "This is the most perfect, and chief science, that sacred, and subtler kind of philosophy, and lastly the most absolute perfection of all most excellent philosophy."[4]

Agrippa was trapped in a superstitious and bigoted age, and so he felt compelled to include a disclaimer: "Wherefore, whatsoever things have here already, and shall afterwards be said by me, I would not have anyone assent to them, nor shall I myself, any further than they shall be approved of by the universal Church, and the congregation of the faithful."[5] It made little difference. Agrippa was condemned and persecuted as a black magician for the major part of his adult life, and his youthful defense of magic only confirmed the suspicions of his critics.

A. E. Waite

Arthur Edward Waite made an attempt to examine the confusion between white magic and black magic in his *Book of Ceremonial Magic* (1911):

> White Ceremonial Magic is, by the terms of its definition, an attempt to communicate with Good Spirits for a good, or at least an innocent, purpose. Black Magic is the attempt to communicate with Evil Spirits for an evil, or for any, purpose.
>
> The contrasts here established seem on the surface perfectly clear. When we come, however, to compare the ceremonial literature of the two classes, we shall find that the distinction is by no means so sharp as might be inferred from the definitions. In the first place, so-called Theurgic Ceremonial, under the pretence of White Magic, usually includes the Rites for the invocation of Evil Spirits. Supposing that they are so invoked for the enforced performance of works contrary to their nature, the issue becomes complicated at once, and White Magic must then be defined as the attempt to communicate with Good or Evil Spirits for a good, or at least for an innocent, purpose. This, of course, still leaves a tolerably clear distinction, though not one that I should admit, if I admitted the practical side of the entire subject to anything but unconditional condemnation. Yet the alternative between a good and an innocent object contains all the material for a further confusion. It will be made clear as I proceed that the purposes and ambitions of Magic are commonly very childish, so that we must

distinguish really between Black and White Magic, not as between the essentially good and evil, but as between that which is certainly evil and that which may only be foolish. Nor does this exhaust the difficulty. As will also be made evident in proceeding, White Ceremonial Magic seems to admit of a number of intentions which are objectionable, as well as many that are frivolous. Hence it must be inferred that there is no very sharp distinction between the two branches of the Art. It cannot be said, even, that Black Magic is invariably and White Magic occasionally evil. What is called Black Magic is by no means diabolical invariably; it is almost as much concerned with preposterous and stupid processes as the White variety with those of an accursed kind. Thus, the most which can be stated is that the literature falls chiefly into two classes, one of which usually terms itself Black, but that they overlap one another.[6]

SACRED MAGIC OF ABRAMELIN

Waite probably had in mind the grimoire known as *The Book of the Sacred Magic of Abramelin the Mage*, which in 1898 had been translated into English from an imperfect French manuscript by S. L. MacGregor Mathers, the magical leader of the Hermetic Order of the Golden Dawn, a Rosicrucian society to which Waite belonged for a time. The *Abramelin* grimoire is superficially a book of white magic, in that it is primarily concerned with establishing communication with the tutelary spirit known in the text as the holy guardian angel, for the purpose of spiritual enlightenment. However, the third book in the Mathers edition of the work contains a series of charms in the form of magic squares of numbers, some of which are intended for purposes that may only be described as black magic.

For example, the first square of the eighth chapter of Book Three is intended "to cause Hail,"[7] a well-known trick attributed to witches by the demonologists of the Church. The squares of the thirteenth chapter of this book are intended "to cause a Dead Body to revive, and perform all the functions which a living person would do."[8] The revival of corpses has historically been classed as black magic.

THEURGIA AND GOETIA

The attempt to communicate with good spirits went under the general term *theurgia* (god work), whereas the attempt to enlist the aid of evil spirits was known as *goetia* (from the Greek for "howling"). An illustration of how well confused these two branches of magic were in late medieval and Renaissance times is the title of the second grimoire in the important British Library occult manuscript known as Sloane 2731. The second tract bears the title *Theurgia Goetia*. The anonymous author of the work wrote of the spirits referred to in the text: "These is by Nature good & Evil that is the one part is good and the other part is Evil."[9]

HIGH AND LOW MAGIC

The distinction between black and white magic, which is fairly modern, is not to be confused with the somewhat older distinction between high magic and low magic. High magic is the intellectual and scholarly magic of Latin or Greek incantations and complex magic circles and sigils, whereas low magic is the magic of simple charms and herbs.

In very general terms, it is the difference between the book magic of the wizard and the folk magic of the witch. Both high magic and low magic may be worked for good or evil purposes.

Historically, practitioners of low or folk magic suffered greater persecution than those who affected the arts of high magic. The lower social classes of Europe were uneducated and poor, ill-equipped to defend themselves in a court of law or from the accusations of the Inquisition. High magic required education. Some mathematical skills were necessary, as well as the reading of Latin at a minimum. These skills were usually only possessed by the upper classes, who could better deflect the ire of the state and the Church. This is the reason Cornelius Agrippa was not burned as a magician, and John Dee was never hanged. Both were able to defend themselves legally. Ignorant rural women were not so fortunate.

THE GRIMOIRES

A study of the grimoires of magic reveals something surprising. In spite of all the talk in the works of Christian demonologists about evil magic in its various forms, the grimoires themselves contain precious little. Here and there you will find spells to work harm on others, but there is no trace of the famous black mass or of the sacrificial murder of infants, which were supposed by the demonologists of the Church to be common practices.

It is true, parts of corpses and things associated with corpses were sometimes required in the grimoires, but nobody was physically harmed to obtain them, although the families of the dead were no doubt outraged by the desecrations. Outright poisons intended to kill are rarely to be discovered in the magical books, in spite of the frequent accusations that witches had recourse to poisons.

The *Goetia*, one of the most infamous of grimoires that is the first tract in the British Library manuscript Sloane 2731, contains instructions on how to contact and command the demons of hell, but their works as described in the text are mostly benign. For example, Bael, the first of the seventy-two demons, is said to confer invisibility. The second, Agares, is somewhat more sinister in that he can cause earthquakes, but of the third, Vassago, it is said: "This Spirit is of a Good Nature."[10] His office is to declare the future and to reveal the locations of things hidden—hardly sinister in itself.

BLACK MASS

The black mass was a fanciful invention of Church writers. It was supposed to be a perversion of the Christian mass, intended to appeal to the Devil by defiling holy things such as the host, which was sometimes to be shoved up the anus of a woman on the altar just before the defrocked priest had sexual connection with her. In place of the wine, the blood of an infant was said to be used. The words of the mass were spoken backwards, and the cross was inverted.

Concerning the historical reality of the black mass, Rossell Hope Robbins wrote:

> Every witches' sabbat was supposed to include a diabolical service, but the "black mass" as such is not found in any contemporary account of witchcraft... the black mass, as something that historically occurred,

is one of the biggest intellectual frauds ever imposed on the lay public.[11]

It is not certain that a true black mass in the fullest sense was ever conducted anywhere. It is likely that some noble patrons seeking benefits from black magic induced priests to defile Christian ceremonies on rare occasions. There are historical accounts to this effect that may be true. If the black mass was ever actually performed, it was a very rare event, and was probably inspired by earlier references to it in the writings of Christian demonologists. For example, the infamous Hellfire Club of England, which met from 1746 to around 1760, is said to have conducted mock black masses, but these were designed to titillate and sexually arouse its members, not to raise magical power.

BLACK PACT

The supposed pacts with the Devil are also much more rare than the literature of the demonologists would suggest. Some pacts were forged by the Inquisition, as a way of damning those accused of witchcraft or necromancy. A few have survived and are curious documents, since they contain the actual signatures of various demons—or at least, what the Inquisition claimed to be the actual signatures.

It is possible that a few magicians may have signed pacts, drawn up by themselves of course, as a way of enlisting the dark magic of hell in pursuit of their personal goals. If so, it was as rare as the performance of the true black mass—which is to say, if it took place at all, it was almost never. But it would be remiss of me to state categorically that the signing of black pacts never took place, since it is impossible to know this with assurance.

CHRISTIAN FUNDAMENTALISM

The view of Christian fundamentalists in the United States today is very similar to that of Kramer and Sprenger in the late 15th century. They take the view that all magic is inherently evil. Since this is manifestly not so, their opinion carries little weight. Only those who believe, as the medieval Church authorities believed, that all things pagan are evil, can presume to condemn magic in a universal way. Satan is regarded as a mental aberration of Christians by most witches and magicians, and is neither worshipped nor invoked.

There is no doubt that devout fundamentalist Christians would happily burn modern Wiccans alive in the name of God and love. Preachers spend much of their time denouncing the evils of New Age beliefs and practices, and telling those who buy books on occultism that they are surely going to hell. Since these preachers are largely powerless to do harm, modern pagans, witches, and magicians tend to look upon them with amused contempt. It is the blessing of our age that science does not recognize the reality of magic. Because the very reality of magic is denied, none of its works are taken seriously by the scientifically minded, and modern magicians and witches are left in peace to practice their art and craft as they will.

CHURCH OF SATAN

The exception to the general disregard of the Devil by modern magicians is found among the members of the Church of Satan, an occult church started by Anton Szandor LaVey (1930–97) in San Francisco in 1966, on the eve of the hippie era of peace and love, mostly as a way of making money. LaVey deliberately constructed his church to outrage Christians, with the hope that the urge to rebel against established authority and the sexual attraction of supposed evil would multiply its membership.

He developed a philosophy that is in part based on the teachings of Aleister Crowley, whose famous dictum was, "Do what thou wilt shall be the whole of the Law." [12] LaVey's brand of Satanism involved sexual freedom and the unrestrained expression of personal desires and urges. It was more hedonistic than devilish.

LaVey created a kind of black mass that was an imitation of the myth of the black mass described in literature. It has no historical basis whatsoever. LaVey himself did not even believe in the existence of Satan, which shows that he was more enlightened than his fundamentalist critics. He did, however, come to realize that magic has power, and in later years began to take the practices of his church more seriously. He came to believe that ritual magic, even in the debased form practiced by his followers, could be the means for obtaining personal desires and goals.

The practices of members of the Church of Satan are not so much evil as they are selfish and vulgar. No babies are sacrificed, but perhaps an occasional virgin gives up her hymen on the altar. It is a kind of play-acting at magic, which nonetheless is able to call up real magical energy at times in spite of its absurdity.

Notes

1. Kramer, p. 20.

2. Ibid., p. 2.

3. James, p. 230.

4. Agrippa, p. 5.

5. Ibid., p. 3.

6. Waite, *Ceremonial Magic*, pp. 14–16.

7. Mathers, *Abramelin*, p. 186.

8. Ibid., p. 196.

9. White, p. 24.

10. Crowley, *Goetia*, p. 28.

11. Robbins, p. 50.

12. Crowley, *Book of the Law*, pp. 18–19.

13

The Book of Spirits

There is a unique object in Western magic that has no parallel. It is known as the book of spirits. What makes it special is that it is not merely a book describing spirits, or the manner of invoking spirits, but a talisman that compels the presence and obedience of spirits. The book of spirits itself has magic power over the incorporeal beings it represents.

It is important not to confuse the book of spirits with three other types of magic books that are used in Western occultism: the grimoire, the book of shadows, and the magical diary.

The grimoires are books that contain rituals and magic procedures, such as the manufacture of magic instruments and talismans, as well as descriptions of spirits and the manner of calling them forth. The true grimoires began as magicians' copy books, in which working magicians recorded their methods as an aid to their memories, and as a legacy for their apprentices. In the 18th and 19th centuries, imitation grimoires were created, usually bearing a false earlier date of publication, and often with authorship attributed to great magicians of the past such as Solomon and Moses.

The book of shadows is a type of book used by witches, in which the magic beliefs and ritual practices of the witch are recorded. The two best known currents of modern witch-craft—Gardnerian witchcraft, named after its founder Gerald B. Gardner, and Alexandrian witchcraft, named after its founder Alex Sanders—both have their own books of cult teachings that are called books of shadows. However, the book of shadows of each individual witch is unique, because it is a record not only of information common to all witches of that esoteric current, but of the personal spell-working and charm-making of that witch.

Similarly, most modern magicians keep a record of ritual work, scrying, and spirit communication. This record book does not have a single acknowledged name, but is called such things as a magic diary or wizard's book. It was from such personal records of practice that the grimoires arose. The wizard's diary and the witch's book of shadows are similar, although the book of shadows may contain more lore of a collective, mythic kind.

The book of spirits is not a grimoire, and not the workbook of a witch or magician—it is an empowered object of immense potency that has the potential to act independent of its maker, or even against his desire, if carelessly handled. Merely to open the book is to summon a spirit. Which spirit is summoned depends on which page is opened. There is no requirement for elaborate rituals in order to use the book. Indeed, the greatest ritual care must be taken to seal and ward the book so that it cannot cause spirits to manifest spontaneously.

We have very precise, practical instructions on the making of the book of spirits. The grimoire known as the *Fourth Book of Occult Philosophy*, attributed (probably falsely) to the magician Henry Cornelius Agrippa, has this to say on the subject:

> There is extant amongst those magicians (who do most use the ministry of evil spirits) a certain rite of invocating spirits by a book to be consecrated before to that purpose; which is properly called, A Book of Spirits (*Liber Spirituum*); whereof we shall now speak a few words. For this book is to be consecrated, a book of evil spirits, ceremoniously to be composed, in their name and order: whereunto they bind with a certain holy oath, the ready and present obedience of the spirits therein written.
>
> Now this book is to be made of most pure and clean paper, that hath never been used before; which many do call virgin paper. And this book must be inscribed after this manner: that is to say, let there be placed on the left side the image of the spirit, and on the right side his character, with the oath above it, containing the name of the spirit, and his dignity and place, with his office and power. Yet very many do compose this book otherwise, omitting the characters or image: but it is more efficacious not to neglect any thing which conduceth to it.
>
> Moreover, there is to be observed the circumstances of places, times, hours, according to the stars which

these spirits are under, and are seen to agree unto, their site, rite, and order being applied.

Which book being so written, and well bound, is to be adorned, garnished, and kept secure, with registers and seals, lest it should happen after the consecration to open in some place not intended, and endanger the operator. Furthermore, this book ought to be kept as reverently as may be: for irreverence of mind causeth it to lose its virtue, with pollution and profanation.

Now this sacred book being thus composed according to the manner already delivered, we are then to proceed to the consecration thereof after a twofold way: one whereof is, that all and singular the spirits who are written in the book, be called to the circle, according to the rites and order which we have before taught; and the book that is to be consecrated, let it be placed without the circle in a triangle. And in the first place, let there be read in the presence of the spirits all the oaths which are written in that book; and then the book to be consecrated being placed without the circle in a triangle there drawn, let all the spirits be compelled to impose their hands where their images and characters are drawn, and to confirm and consecrate the same with a special and common oath. Which being done, let the book be taken and shut, and preserved as we have before spoken, and let the spirits be licensed to depart, according to due rite and order.

There is another manner of consecrating a book of spirits, which is more easy, and of much efficacy to produce every effect, except that in opening this book the spirits do not always come visible. And this way is thus: let there be made a book of spirits as we have before set forth; but in the end thereof let there be written invocations and bonds, and strong conjurations, wherewith every spirit may be bound. Then this book must be bound between two tables or lamens, and in the inside thereof let there be drawn the holy pentacles of the Divine Majesty, which we have before set forth and described out of the *Apocalypse*: then let the first of them be placed in the beginning of the book, and the second at the end of the same.

This book being perfected after this manner, let it be brought in a clear and fair time, to a circle prepared in a crossway, according to the art which we have before delivered; and there in the first place the book being opened, let it be consecrated to the rites and ways which we have before declared concerning consecration. Which being done, let all the spirits be called which are written in the book, in their own order and place, by conjuring them thrice by the bonds described in the book, that they come unto that place within the space of three days, to assure their obedience, and confirm the same, to the book so to be consecrated. Then let the book be wrapped up in clean linen, and buried in the middle of the circle, and there fast stopped up: and then the circle being destroyed, after the spirits are licensed, depart before the rising of the sun: and on the third day, about the middle of the night, return, and new-make the circle, and with bended knees make prayer and giving thanks unto God, and let a precious perfume be made, and open the hole, and take out the book; and so let it be kept, not opening the same. Then you shall license the spirits in their order, and destroying the circle, depart before the sunrise. And this is the last rite and manner of consecrating, profitable to whatsoever writings and experiments, which do direct to spirits, placing the same between two holy lamens or pentacles, as before is shown.

But the operator, when he would work by the book thus consecrated, let him do it in a fair and clear season, when the spirits are least troubled; and let him place himself towards the region of the spirits. Then let him open the book under a due register; let him invoke the spirits by their oath there described and confirmed, and by the name of their character and image, to that purpose which you desire: and, if there be need, conjure them by the bonds placed in the end of the book. And having attained your desired effect, then you shall license the spirits to depart.[1]

The first thing to notice in this excerpt is that the writer of the *Fourth Book* asserts that the book of spirits is a way of binding and compelling evil spirits. He says nothing about good spirits or those that are of indifferent moral qualities. This is shortsighted, in my opinion. There is no reason why this excellent magical device cannot be used to summon and direct more benevolent spiritual beings. The same principles apply whether the spirits hold helpful or harmful intentions.

The book is to be made of clean paper—in past centuries writing surfaces were expensive, and were often written over twice with the text crossing at right angles, or erased and written upon a second time. That is all the term "virgin paper" means in this context, paper that has never before been written on. Most modern paper is virgin paper, but beware of recycled paper, which should not be used for the book of spirits.

The book is so constructed that when opened to any place and laid flat, on the left page is the detailed image of a particular spirit, showing the attributes of that spirit, and on the right page the sigil of that spirit, along with the oath the spirit has sworn to obey. The oath contains the name of the spirit, its rank or hierarchy (duke, earl, prince, king, etc.), its place in the world (east, west, north, or south), and its office or function. Any distinguishing characteristic or association of the spirit should be mentioned in this oath, to further identify and bind the spirit.

By this manner of construction, the mere opening of the book is an invocation to the spirit whose image and sigil are exposed to the light. It is equivalent to opening an astral portal that is keyed to this spirit and no other spirit.

The sigil of the spirit is a kind of graphic signature that may be psychically revealed to the magician when he meditates upon the spirit, or summons the spirit ritually; or it may be generated by a system of sigil generation that is empowered by astrological, numerological, and magical correspondences. The method of generating sigils on the sigil-rose of the Golden Dawn, or Kabbalistically using the Aiq-Beker (Kabbalah of Nine Chambers), are two examples of the latter method of sigil generation. In my opinion, sigils are more personal and more potent when received psychically. However, it is easier to generate a large set of sigils using a method of mechanical sigil-making, which has the virtue of producing a set of sigils that are uniform and harmonious in appearance.

In the making of the book, auspicious astrological times should be observed. Each spirit has its own favorable hour of the day and day of the week, as well as favorable patterns of the heavens under which its power is enhanced and exalted. When drawing and painting the image of a spirit, take note of what times are best for the enhancement of the spirit's working, and create its image at those times and under those stars and planets.

After the book has been completed and you wish to call upon the spirit, again it is best to mark its auspicious astrological times and to call it forth from the book when it is at its greatest potency, according to the harmonies of the heavens. It will find these times more conducive to its functioning, and it will be more effective in its work. The author speaks of a "fair and clear season" when the spirits are "least troubled." The main consideration is wind, which disturbs the atmosphere and makes spirit manifestation more difficult. Spirits are best called when the air is quiet and of a moderate temperature.

The pages of the book, thus painted and inscribed under favorable stars and at favorable hours, are bound together between two stout covers, and also between seals of power that act as barriers to the passage of the spirits occupying the pages of the book. It is possible to bind blank pages into a book and then inscribe them already joined, but if an error is made the entire book is tainted, whereas if the pages are written and painted first, an error is only fatal to the single leaf of the book upon which it occurs.

The seals or wards that guard the front and back of the book against the passage of the spirits are the names or personal symbols of higher spirits or gods that have authority over the spirits in the book. For example, the Alpha and the Omega of Jesus Christ that is mentioned in Revelation 1:11 might be used: the Greek letter Alpha on the front cover, and the Greek letter Omega on the back cover. Or the Tetragrammaton of Hebrew letters, the most holy name of God, with the first two letters on the front cover and the final two on the back cover. Symbols from Revelation are mentioned by the author of the *Fourth Book* as having power to ward these spirits. These would include such complex symbols as the vision of Christ amidst the seven gold candlesticks, with seven stars in his right hand and a sword coming from his mouth (Revelation 1:12–16), or the vision of the Queen of Heaven (Revelation 12:1).

Additional seals and names may be placed on the insides of the covers, on the spine, and on the edges of the book to seal the edges. It is useful that the covers of the book be constructed in such a way that they fold over the edges, enclosing the pages entirely. The author mentions "registers" to guard the book. This term is somewhat obscure to modern readers, but is an old term for the ribbons bound into the spine of books that were used as bookmarks. The author means that the magician should take care to mark well which page he wishes to open by means of a bookmark, so that he does not open the book to the wrong page in error.

The book is empowered or activated by drawing a ritual circle, and beside it a triangle of evocation. The triangle is equilateral, points away from the circle, is three feet long on each side, and two feet away from the edge of the circle—so specifies the grimoire known as the *Goetia* (British Library MS. Sloane 2731). According to the author of the *Fourth Book of Occult Philosophy*, the magician first reads all the oaths from the book while holding it in his hands as he stands within the protective circle. He then places the book into the triangle of evocation and has each spirit lay its hand on its individual pages and confirm its obedience with a common oath. This would be something short and simple, such as:

"I, [name of spirit], do swear my obedience to the matters written upon this page in this book."

It is to be presumed that the magician would stand within the circle with a sword, and use the tip of the sword to turn the pages of the book as he successively summoned each spirit and instructed it to lay its hand on the open pages that bear its image and sigil, and swear obedience to the oath inscribed there. It is dangerous for the magician to break the circle when dealing with spirits, particularly evil spirits, so he would be well advised to slide the book from the circle into the triangle using the point of his sword, after he has finished reading aloud the oaths written on its pages. However, the author of the *Fourth Book* neglects to give these judicious warnings.

A second method for empowering the book of spirits mentioned by pseudo-Agrippa is to call the spirits to a circle drawn on a crossroads at night in some little-traveled location, and instruct the spirits to swear their obedience to the book over a three-day period while the book remains wrapped in clean linen and buried under the ground at the crossroads. After three days, the magician returns, redraws the circle that he erased to avoid detection, and digs up the consecrated and energized book. This second method has the advantage of not requiring the magician to witness each individual spirit swear its oath of obedience on each set of facing pages. It has the disadvantage of requiring the use of a deserted crossroads, which is increasingly difficult to find. Our author also states that when this second method is used, the spirits called forth do not always come to visible appearance, suggesting that it is a less potent method.

Occupying the end of the second form of the book, after the pages that bear the images and sigils of the spirits, are the bonds. These are dread curses that are to be spoken only if the spirits of the book fail to appear promptly when called. You will find specimens of this type of binding at the end of the grimoire known as the *Goetia*, which is of course a general pattern for a book of spirits. As a matter of interest, I will give the curse known as the Spirits' Chain:

O thou wicked and disobedient Spirit N., because thou hast rebelled, and hast not obeyed nor regarded my words which I have rehearsed; they being all glorious and incomprehensible names of the true God, the maker and creator of thee and of me, and of all the world; I do by the power of these names the which no creature is able to resist, curse thee into the depths of the Bottomless Abyss, there to remain until the Day of Doom in chains, and in fire and brimstone unquenchable, unless thou forthwith appear here and before this Circle, in this triangle to do my will. And therefore, come thou quickly and peaceably, in and by these names of God, Adonai, Zabaoth, Adonai, Amioran; come thou! come thou! for it is the King of Kings, even Adonai, who commandeth thee.[2]

Notice that the magician assumes the identity of Adonai in speaking this bond. It is only by becoming God that the magician can speak with the power and authority of God. He takes on the nature of Adonai, as he understands it, in a kind of inspired possession, allowing the authority of Adonai to flow through him and energize his words. It is not a trick—or at least, if it is a trick, it is the magician who tricks himself into believing that he has become the emissary and the very speaking mouth of Adonai.

The book of spirits is to be encountered in many forms in Western magic, but the basic elements remain constant. The spirits are called forth to swear obedience upon their names and symbols, which are recorded. For example, in the grimoire known as the *Book of the Sacred Magic of Abramelin the Mage*, the book is not actually composed of pages, but of sand:

And when the Spirits shall have appeared, you shall command them in no way to quit the place, until they shall have manifested unto you the Symbol of the Operation which you desire, together with the Names of the Spirits capable of putting the same into execution, together with their Symbols. And then you shall see the Prince unto whom the Operation appeartaineth avow, write, and sign upon the Sand the Symbol, together with the Name of the Spirit who is to serve for this Operation. Then shall you take the Surety and Oath of the Prince upon the Symbol, and also of his Ministers, as you will have previously done in accordance with the (directions given in the) Fourteenth Chapter. And should several Symbols be given, make them take Oath upon them all. This being done, you can dismiss them in the manner we have already described, taking heed before this to copy the Symbols which they shall have traced upon the Sand, because in departing they will destroy the same.[3]

It is not uncommon that the spirits are made to sign their names or their sigils in the book beneath the oaths to which they are bound, after the manner of the signing of a legal contract. Since spirits are not corporeal, even though they can appear completely solid and made of flesh to the five senses of those who perceive them, various methods for receiving the signatures and sigils of spirits are used. In addition to having the spirits make marks in a floor of fine sand, a silver plate was used by the author of *Abramelin*,[4] upon which the holy guardian angel of the magician inscribed his sigil. Spirits are capable of possessing the body of the magician, sometimes without his awareness or memory of ever being possessed, and while they control his body, they can use it to write their names and draw their sigils with his hand. Possession is often responsible for the seemingly miraculous reception of spirit sigils. Temporary spirit possession occurs more often than most people would dare to imagine.

We will end this short examination of the book of spirits by mentioning that the infamous black pact, wherein a witch or magician swears obedience to the Devil, is nothing but the book of spirits in reverse. Instead of an evil spirit swearing an oath of obedience upon a book that bears its signature and sign, the wretched witch or necromancer swears obedience to Satan, and either writes his name, or makes his mark, in his own blood at the foot of the oath in the Devil's black book. The black book of hell is thus a book of men and women who are bound to him, and who do him service—the exact reverse of the magician's book of spirits.

NOTES

1. Agrippa, *Fourth Book*, pp. 93–95.

2. Crowley, *Goetia*, pp. 85–86.

3. Mathers, *Abramelin*, pp. 134–35.

4. Ibid., p. 82.

14

Esoteric Energy

When those involved in spiritual or magical pursuits speak or write about occult energy, esoteric energy, or magical energy, the materially minded are apt to mock them. "Where is this energy?" they demand. "Why can't we measure it with instruments? It is not energy at all. What physical work does it accomplish?"

In a narrow sense, they are correct. Magic cannot directly cause physical effects, in a brute-force kind of way, although physical effects result from it indirectly. The energies that are discussed in connection with magic cannot be measured or recorded by machines.

This being so, are they even energies? In the broader definition of the word, yes, they are energies. *Webster's New World Dictionary* defines energy as "potential forces; inherent power; capacity for vigorous action" in addition to the stricter scientific definition, "the capacity for doing work."

Mana

There is a Polynesian word for this esoteric energy. *Mana.*
It should not be confused with the similarly pronounced
word *manna*, which is supposed to be a miraculous food
supplied by God. Mana with a single *n* is described by *Webster's* as "an impersonal supernatural force." It is impersonal in the sense that electricity is impersonal. Electricity
is a form of energy without intentions or preferences. It is
mindless and soulless, neither good nor bad, and can be
channeled and directed by anyone for any purpose.

Mana can be channeled for both good and evil purposes,
since it has no will or mind of its own. It is raw occult potential.

Since the Polynesian word is unique, and specifically
describes magical energy, it would seem reasonable to use it,
but for some reason it has not come into common use in the
West, where the much less specific term *energy* is used in its
place. In order to distinguish the energy of magic from the
energy of physical action, it is necessary to qualify it with an
adjective, such as occult, esoteric, or magical energy.

Power of change

Occult energy does possess the potential to cause significant changes indirectly, both in the human organism, and as
magicians assert, on the higher, esoteric planes of reality. It
can modify the thoughts, the emotions, and the sensations,
and even affect the general health of the mind and body. On
the astral level it can change entire environments, and can
both create and destroy intelligent spiritual beings.

It should be obvious that magical energy can cause
change—how else are we to explain the persistence of mag-

ical activity down through the entire course of human history, in every human society on the planet? Unless magic did something, it seems unlikely that it would be the life-work of countless individuals, who made it their careers and even their spiritual callings.

In order to examine this topic, we do not necessarily need to assume that any changes brought about by magical energies are grossly physical in nature, but we must acknowledge that magic brings about changes that are perceived and experienced by those who practice it, and often by those at whom it is directed. If shamans and their patients did not believe that magic was accomplishing changes to their reality, they would not hold it in such high esteem.

SUBJECTIVE AND OBJECTIVE CHANGE

Magical energy often effects change in a subjective manner. Change is perceived following a ritual of magic by those involved with the working of the ritual. Other human beings who may be in the general area, but are not involved with the ritual, may fail to perceive any differences.

We might say that magical change is inward change, but this is simplistic and misleading. Those who perceive the working of esoteric energies see changes not only within their own bodies and minds, but in the world around them.

A psychologist might suggest that they are merely projecting their delusions. Yet for each of us, our entire world is a creation of our mind. There is no such thing as "us" and the "greater universe"—no division between the two exists, because we create our greater universe within our mind,

even as we create our memories and our personality and
our sense of self.

To a magician, the power of magic is not imposed on
the so-called outer world. No, when a ritual is worked effectively, that outer world actually changes. A stranger may not
always be able to perceive the transformations, but they are
absolutely real and tangible to those who do perceive them.

This naturally has given rise to great confusion. A magician may see a transformation in his environment as the
result of working a ritual, but a person in the same place who
is not involved in the magic may see no difference at all, and
may scoff at the idea that the magic has accomplished anything. The confusion is only increased when attempts are
made to measure the force of magic with physical machines,
since invariably this results in failure.

THREE STAGES OF ENERGY MANIPULATION

Magic involves the manipulation of this esoteric or nonphysical energy. An act of magic has three stages, from this
subjective point of view: the accumulation of energy, the
shaping or filtering of energy for a specific purpose, and the
sending or directing of that energy to its fulfillment.

Esoteric energy is accumulated by focusing the mind on
a specific purpose, and using the emotions to heighten the
strength and prolong the duration of that mental focus. The
result is a change in consciousness from the everyday awareness to an elevated or altered state of mind. Sometimes stress
is applied to the body for the same reason, to concentrate
and alter the consciousness. Sexual energy may be employed,
or the sacrifice of blood, when very intense energies are
required.

Once the energy has been accumulated, it is shaped or filtered by the use of a dramatic enactment of the realization of the purpose for which the ritual is being worked, using symbolic representations of the various aspects of the purpose. This may be an actual physical acting out of a small dramatic scenario, or it may involve only the simple manipulation of a symbolic object or objects.

At the climax of the dramatic enactment of the fulfillment of the purpose, the accumulated and filtered energy is released and sent to accomplish the magical desire. This is very much like a sexual climax, in that the tension built up in the mind and body is suddenly relaxed and forgotten. It is like the tension in a bent wand that is allowed to spring back straight, leaving no trace of its former curved condition.

Esoteric energy in image magic

As an historical example of these three stages in the ritual use of esoteric force, we may examine the ancient and widespread practice of causing pain or death to an enemy by means of a small doll or image of the enemy. In England this witch doll was known as a poppet.

The witch would construct the doll, binding into it strands of hair from the head of the enemy it was intended to represent and embody, or threads from his garments, or fingernail clippings—anything closely in contact with the person or closely related to the person.

During the ritual, hatred and malice would be directed at the person the doll represented, through the medium of the doll. This stage corresponded to the subjective accumulation of esoteric energy.

The filtering or shaping of the energy was completed by naming the doll with the name of the intended victim of the ritual. Sometimes a mock baptism was used to give the name more force, and make the identification between the name and the doll more perfect. By this act, the hatred of the witch was provided with a specific target.

The release of the esoteric potential was marked by some decisive physical action, such as the thrusting of a long pin or nail through the torso of the doll, in the heart region. The heart was believed to be one of the seats of life in the body. Often these dolls were thrust through not merely with a single nail, but with many nails—yet one of them was the decisive thrust, the stroke that caused the malice to take its effect on the victim. It was necessary for the witch to say, in some symbolic manner, "So let it be accomplished!" This was not always done with words, but might be done by a physical action.

It was the general custom to leave such dolls on a ledge in the chimney over the smoke of the fireplace, where the soul linked to the doll would be ceaselessly tormented by the heat from the fire. Numerous examples have been discovered in old European chimneys of not only dolls but also hearts, lemons, and (of all things) onions stuck full of nails and pins.[1]

Before anyone accuses me of prejudice against witches, let me add that most European witches of the Middle Ages and the Renaissance were not evil—but neither were all of them always entirely good. On occasion, some of them did use magic for malicious purposes. These little chimney treasures are proof of that malice.

PSYCHIC ENERGY

Esoteric energy must not be confused with psychic energy. It is much more than the mere power of the individual mind or brain. Esoteric energy has its origin outside the personality, or lower self. Even though esoteric energy is perceived, subjectively, to flow from the magician when it is liberated during ritual, this is an illusion—it actually is tapped and flows from a more mysterious and impersonal source.

A psychic may be able to affect another human being by concentrating on that person, using telepathy or psycho-kinesis, but such psychic powers are not magic, and do not involve esoteric or magical energy. It should be possible to measure the energy of psychokinesis directly by machines. This is never possible for magical energy, or mana, which manifests in physical ways only indirectly. The power of magic is nonphysical, and the effects of magical energy are subtle.

Eventually, it may become possible for science to study and measure psychic energy, and even to harness it. This will never be the case for esoteric energy, which is forever separate and apart from the realm of science.

PROBABILITY SHIFT

It is my own belief that raw magical force works by changing probability. It causes unlikely events to happen. There is no way to measure this shift in probability by material instruments. Only the effect of the change, the unlikely event that occurs due to the probability shift, can be physically investigated and recorded.

When a magician concentrates mental and emotional energy on a purpose, it primes the pump, allowing access to a much larger reservoir of esoteric potential, the power of which is greatly beyond the extent of the power of the individual magician. In this way, a magician can do things that are miraculous, although they usually appear to observers to be no more than curious coincidences.

Through magic, individual consciousness can tap into universal mind. The blind force of this higher mind, which is impersonal and unconscious in the human sense, can be channeled for the lower purposes of the individual human ego. Amazing physical changes may occur, either in a secondary way through the actions of human beings who have been motivated by the magic, or in a direct way that appears to observers to be no more than luck.

To the magician who taps into this higher source, the power seems to flow from his own will and intention, but this is an illusion. He merely directs the working of the energy; his ego-personality does not originate it.

MIRACULOUS EFFECTS

It is rare that the liberation of this higher esoteric energy causes material events that seem to directly defy the laws of physics, but there are enough accounts of such things happening that we must credit the possibility of such events. For example, there are many claims that acts of faith have caused the spontaneous disappearance of cancerous tumors or skin ulcers. If such remissions do occur, they would give the appearance of the direct working of mana, or esoteric energy, on the physical world.

Yet, even in these cases, what occurs is not strictly impossible on the molecular level, but only extraordinarily improbable. Such a remission is so improbable, that for all practical purposes it is regarded as impossible—but if all the cells in a cancerous tumor were suddenly to die over a very brief period, and the growth of healthy tissue were to accelerate to replace their loss, such a spontaneous remission could occur.

Levitation is another example. We are surrounded by molecules of air, which strike our skin on all sides in a random way. There is no reason why, at any given time, these molecules should not strike us more often on the soles of our feet than on other parts of our body, and if this happened, we would be lifted into the air by this upward pressure.

It would not require any psychic force on our part to achieve this levitation, or any physical exertion of any kind. Indeed, this change in probability, in itself, would not be measurable in any direct manner. Yet it is not impossible—only very, very unlikely. But there is no physical reason why it could not occur in the next minute. It may be the explanation for some of the historical accounts of levitation among Christian saints and Eastern mystics.

THE DIVINE SOURCE

There is no difference between magic and miracles. Acts that are called miraculous are merely acts of magic that have received the sanction of the established religions of the world. They are attributed to God rather than to human beings, but when a magician taps into the source of esoteric energy, he is tapping into the wellspring of the divine itself, for his own desired purpose. A saint does the same through prayer, and achieves a similar result. Both magician and saint use esoteric energy to cause change, even though their techniques differ.

All true magic is a direct communion between the conscious will of a human being and the impersonal force of the Godhead, the ultimate source of all life and all existence. The difference between the magician and the saint is one of attitude—whereas the saint requests the intervention of the divine, the magician demands it.

This may seem blasphemous to those who are religious, but the magician merely relies on tried and true channels for the power of the divine source of change, and directs the flow of that impersonal power for his own desires. At this highest level of the divine, all differences are merged, all opposites resolved, in what I have termed in some of my books the Unmanifest. There is no divine ego to take offense at the magician's hubris, any more than electricity takes offense at the electrician who causes it to flow through a wire.

Veil of unknowing

With the use of the esoteric energy flowing from the divine source, all things are possible. However, the human mind has protective barriers that prevent casual access to this power. This is a good thing, since without them, the world would probably have been destroyed long ago.

Magicians are able to trick their minds into bypassing these barriers, using age-old tried and tested techniques of ritual, so that a tiny fraction of esoteric energy is liberated from the Unmanifest. A tiny fraction, yet it is enough to work wonders. A man who could liberate this energy at will would be omnipotent, a God incarnate. Some believe that

Jesus was such a man—a magician of great ability who used his gifts for healing.

Jesus is not the only person recorded in ancient histories as having cured the sick and raised the dead to life. The same is said of the sage Apollonius of Tyana, for example. However, because the Christian churches recognize the miracles of Jesus and reject those of Apollonius, Jesus is called divine, and Apollonius is known only as a magician. The acts of many such magicians were set down by the ancient chroniclers.

Cosmic trigger

There is a mistaken belief that it requires great exertion to liberate this esoteric energy. This error is due to the willful and intense excitation of the emotions that usually accompanies works of magic. Magicians inflame their desire during rituals, but they do so not because it is required to tap into the divine source of power, but because it is a proven method for tricking the mind into dropping the protective barriers that screen that source of energy from our awareness, if only for the briefest of instants. Excitation produces exhaustion and forgetfulness of self.

Most magicians operate under the false notion that the power of magic is this intense inner excitation of the emotions. They do not realize that the arousal of their emotions is merely a prelude to the liberation of the true power of magic, which is external and separate from their ego-identity.

Almost all of the emotional energy raised during ritual by various means, such as sexual arousal or blood sacrifice, is wasted. Only a tiny fraction of it serves to prime the pump of the divine source, so that esoteric energy can flow down and shift probability in favor of the realization of the ritual desire. It is a kind of cosmic trigger, so to speak, that fires the gun of the Unmanifest, a trigger requiring only the lightest of pressures.

Because this trigger is very difficult to reach, magic is notoriously unreliable. Sometimes it works, sometimes it does not, and sometimes it seems not to work when it actually does—but it works in such unexpected ways that its working goes unrecognized. The surest way to fail in magic is to announce to the world exactly what you intend to achieve ahead of time.

The unconscious mind must be tickled open by ritual, and tricked into lowering its veil of ignorance so that the light of the Unmanifest can shine through the crack. This is a technique of the mind and emotions that all magicians must learn through trial and error. It is like looking at a very faint star—if you stare directly at it, the star vanishes, but if you look to the side, it can be observed with a shift of the attention, yet without moving the eyes.

SEA OF POSSIBILITIES

The things that esoteric energy can be made to accomplish are endless in number and stagger the imagination in their scope. Even the greatest of magicians, such as a Jesus or an Apollonius, have achieved only a tiny fraction of what is possible.

There exists a Kabbalistic fable that the speaking of the true name of God, in its correct order of letters and with the accurate pronunciation, would bring the entire universe to its end.

This fable indicates the full potential of the divine source of power that may be tapped using the methods of magic, if only the inherent barriers that exist in the mind could be circumvented. It also suggests the dreaded consequences should any magician succeed in finding a way to consistently bypass those barriers, which have been erected to safeguard our reality. It is both a promise for the future and a warning of things to come.

NOTES

1. Elworthy, pp. 54–55.

15

Spirits' Rights: A Manifesto

THE MANIFESTO

Axiom 1

It is herein asserted as axiomatic, based on direct observation, that spirits who communicate and interact with human beings are self-aware and possess their own strong sense of independent identity.

Axiom 2

It is asserted as axiomatic, based on direct observation, that spirits who communicate and interact with human beings have a capacity for reasoned thought and for moral and ethical behavior of the highest order.

Axiom 3

It is asserted as axiomatic, based on direct observation, that spirits who communicate and interact with human beings experience both happiness and unhappiness, and, furthermore, that they seek out and rejoice in pleasure but shun and are tormented by pain.

Premise

The premise is offered that human beings in communication with spirits may by their emotions, thoughts, and actions either increase the happiness of spirits or decrease it. Specifically, that humans have the ability through willful and deliberate actions to constrain spirits and to cause spirits to suffer.

Argument

An argument is made that as intelligent beings who are self-aware and who have the capacity to experience both pleasure and suffering, spirits are entitled to the same basic rights as humans—life, liberty, and the pursuit of happiness. No one shall seek to deprive spirits of these rights, which have the same source as the rights of humans.

Life for a spirit consists of continued self-aware existence. Liberty consists of the freedom to travel and act without constraint. The pursuit of happiness consists of actions perceived by a spirit as essential to its fulfillment as a conscious, independent being.

Conclusion

The conclusion is reached that spirits, as intelligent and self-aware beings, possess the same inherent dignities as humans, and may demand the same level of civility and respect.

COMMENTARY

It may appear strange that I raise the matter of spirits' rights, when so many in our Western societies stoutly deny the very existence of spiritual beings, but those of us who have interacted directly or indirectly with spirits have no doubt as to their existence, and it is to these more knowledgeable readers that my remarks are mainly directed. I have little hope of affecting the beliefs of those who, without any knowledge of spirits, scorn and dismiss them out of an impulse of sheer social prejudice.

The essential nature of spirits is open to debate. I do not presume to know with certainty what spirits are, where they come from, or what their ultimate purposes may be—however, my direct involvement with these beings has convinced me that they do exist, on some level other than the physical level. When you have conversed with a spirit, shared jokes with that being, listened to the spirit express its hopes and desires and intentions, it is difficult to assert that it does not exist. The question becomes—What is the nature of that existence?

Accepting that spirits exist, it may further be observed that many of them behave as intelligent, independent persons. They possess strong self-identities and have their own likes and dislikes, their individual goals, their own hopes and fears. They are capable of deriving enjoyment from their existence, and are equally subject to unhappiness and suffering when conditions are not to their liking. True, there are spiritual beings of a lower order who do not appear to be intelligent or capable of communication through the use of language, but this manifesto is concerned with those who do exhibit intelligent behavior and who interact with human beings as intellectual equals.

These intelligent spirits may identify themselves as the souls or spirits of human beings who have died. Is this identification accurate? For the purposes of spirits' rights, it does not matter. Other intelligent spirits identify themselves as completely nonhuman beings, and again, in the matter of spirits' rights, it is beside the point how they may see themselves. What matters is how these spirits behave toward human beings. In my experience, most intelligent spirits behave in a civil and moral way. They are polite, compassionate, and loving. They are reasonable and can be reasoned with. It is possible to hold a conversation, and even a debate, with spiritual beings, and those spirits are no more apt to resort to irrational or emotional arguments than human beings.

Given this reasonable and ethical behavior of spirits, it seems to me deplorable that they are regarded in many quarters, even by those who habitually interact with them, as in some way inferior to human beings. The attempt is frequently made to coerce spirits into performing actions against their will. Examples of this behavior are rife throughout the history of Western ceremonial magic. Spirits are treated as servants, or even as slaves, by those who summon them, and are compelled to perform tasks as though they were incorporeal beasts of burden.

When spirits refuse the demands made upon them, they are often threatened with punishment, or even deliberately tormented by various magical means. It was common in centuries past to bind spirits into objects that might be subjected to heat or other unpleasant physical conditions, as a way of torturing the spirits into compliance. One torture was to set the object that served as a spirit's prison above a fire to be roasted; another was to hang it from a tree so that it would sway and twist in the wind; yet another form of torture was to bury the object, so that the spirit was buried alive.

In modern times, few who converse with spirits are aware of these methods of coercion and torture, which evolved in the context of ceremonial magic, but they exhibit an equal disregard for the freedom or happiness of spirits. It is common for spirits to be automatically regarded as demons, even though they have committed no wrong. The immediate response of the average person to a spirit communication is terror. All the prejudices instilled since childhood come bubbling to the surface. They begin to curse the spirit, threaten it, abuse it, make prayers against it, and call in the exorcists. Little wonder the spirit usually withdraws in confusion and disgust.

Even when a continuing communication is sustained with a spirit, there may be a tendency to regard the spirit as a kind of astral pet, rather than as an intelligent equal with as much right to be treated with respect and dignity as any human. Old prejudices die hard. It is a tragedy that a spirit who comes to a human seeking friendship may find only contempt and abuse. Such spirits can scarcely be blamed if they respond with resentment, or even outright malice, and in this way the prejudices perpetuate themselves.

It has become common in Western nations to talk about animal rights. The recognition is growing in our societies that living creatures who have feelings and the capacity to experience both pleasure and pain should be accorded a basic level of honor and dignity, as sensitive fellow creatures with whom we share a common origin.

The time has arrived to raise the bar of universal rights and freedoms to embrace not only sentient physical beings who are nonhuman but those who are nonphysical as well. Unlike animals, spirits can both feel and reason. In this double capacity they are closer to our human nature than the beasts of the field. It is my contention, expressed by this manifesto of spirits' rights, that the basic rights of spiritual beings must be recognized and respected. Spirits are no longer to be treated as slaves or pets, but are to be given all the honors of rational beings.

16

The Enochian
Apocalypse Working

THE UNION OF A SAINT AND A ROGUE

Between the years 1582 and 1589, the Elizabethan scholar
John Dee (1527–1609) conducted a series of ritual communications with a set of discarnate entities who eventually
came to be known as the Enochian angels, because they identified themselves to Dee as the same angels who had taught
the magic of heaven to the biblical patriarch Enoch. It was
Dee's plan to use the complex system of magic communicated by the angels to advance the expansionist policies of his
sovereign, Elizabeth the First. At that time England lay under
the looming shadow of invasion from Spain. Dee hoped to
control the hostile potentates of Europe by using Enochian
magic to command the tutelary spirits that presided over
their various nations.

Dee was a thoroughly remarkable man. Educated at Cambridge and on the Continent, his intellectual brilliance and skill as a magician were both famous and infamous throughout Europe. Not only was he a gifted mathematician, astronomer, and cartographer, but when occasion demanded it he also served the queen as her personal astrologer, occult counselor, and confidential espionage agent.[1] His father, Roland, had held the position of chief steward at the feasting table of Elizabeth's father, King Henry the Eighth, so the family name Dee was well known in the royal court. During the Catholic rule of Henry's daughter, Mary Tudor, both Dee and Elizabeth were arrested and investigated for high treason, and this shared persecution at the hands of Mary forged a close bond of trust between the scholar and the young princess. When Elizabeth ascended to the throne after Mary's death, Dee was given the honor by Robert Dudley of choosing an astrologically auspicious date for her coronation ceremony.

In his occult work, Dee was aided by an equally extraordinary person, Edward Kelley (1555–97), the son of a Worcester apothecary, who dreamed of discovering the secret of the philosopher's stone and dabbled in the forbidden art of necromancy. Kelley attended Oxford but never graduated, then enjoyed a spotted career as a counterfeiter of debased coins, a forger of false title deeds, an alchemist, and a necromancer. It was his quest for alchemical knowledge that brought him to the private library of John Dee in 1582, and it was primarily this obsession that made him agree to serve as Dee's crystal gazer, or *scryer* as they were then called—he hoped Dee would help him to discover the secret of making the fabled red powder of alchemy.

Dee was a saint, Kelley a rogue, but they were bound together by their common fascination for ceremonial magic and the wondrous gifts it promised. Dee himself possessed little talent for mediumship. When he attempted to scry into his crystal globe in private, he achieved some minor success but not enough for his ambitions. He tried to overcome this lack of psychic talent by hiring a former lay preacher named Barnabas Saul as his professional scryer. Although Saul possessed mediumistic gifts, he was frightened by Dee's researches, and when he came under accusation in London for the forbidden practice of spirit invocation, he told Dee he saw nothing more in the crystal and would have to leave Dee's service.

This separation between Dee and Saul occurred at the time of Kelley's arrival at Dee's house in Mortlake, a little village near London. Kelley offered to attempt to scry into Dee's crystal. Dee accepted, little knowing what to expect. Kelley's success was immediate and profound. In minutes he established clear communication with the spirits who would later identify themselves as the angelic teachers of Enoch. When Dee recognized Kelley's considerable psychic abilities, so much greater than those of Barnabas Saul, he eagerly employed Kelley as his seer for the sum of fifty pounds per annum.

Dee invoked the Enochian angels to visible appearance within polished globes of natural rock crystal by means of prayers and certain magical seals, the making of which the angels described to Kelley. The usual practice was for Dee to withdraw himself into a small room off his study, which he called his oratory, to pray and invoke while Kelley remained seated before the scrying stone. After Kelley alerted Dee to the presence of the spirits, Dee would return to his desk and question them with his pen in his hand, ready to write down whatever his seer told him. Kelley reported verbatim the sayings and doings of the angels that he saw in the crystal, and Dee recorded their words and actions in a series of magical diaries.

It is one of the great mysteries of the history of Western occultism that these diaries survived down to the present. Half of them were buried in the ground in a field next to Dee's house, and the other half were hidden in a secret drawer in one of Dee's trunks. Dee kept them hidden because he knew that if they ever became public knowledge, they would destroy his reputation and perhaps cost him his life. It was not illegal to communicate with angels, but it was illegal to communicate with all other types of spirits, which were regarded by the church and state as devilish. Not all the spirits written about in the Enochian diaries are angels.

When Dee died in 1609,[2] many of his possessions, including the trunk, were sold at auction. The diaries in the field were dug up before the wet and the worms destroyed them, but it was only decades later that the diaries in the trunk were discovered, and the two halves of the Enochian record reunited.

The most important portion of Dee's transcription of the Enochian communications covers Dee's work with Kelley during the years 1582–1587. Most of these "workings," as Dee termed them, from 1583 and later, were published in London in 1659 by Meric Casaubon under the title *A True and Faithful Relation of What Passed for Many Yeers Between Dr. John Dee … and Some Spirits*. This fascinating book has been reprinted several times in recent decades and is readily available. It was derived from the diaries buried in the field and later dug up. Earlier scrying sessions with Kelley that took place in 1582, but were not included in Casaubon's book, remained in manuscript form for many years, but have recently been published in *John Dee's Five Books of Mystery*, edited by Joseph H. Peterson. This material comes from the diaries that were hidden in the secret drawer in Dee's trunk.

The spirits who appeared in the crystal get their collective name from the nature of the system of magic they described to Dee. It was, they claimed, the very magic that Enoch the Patriarch learned from them after being lifted up to heaven while still alive. The angel Ave tells Dee: "Now hath it pleased God to deliver this Doctrine again out of darknesse: and to fulfill his promise with thee, for the books of Enoch."[3] Compared to this, the angels asserted to Kelley, all other forms of magic were mere playthings.

Although Dee faithfully recorded all the details of Enochian magic in his diaries, he never tried to work this system in any serious way. We cannot know the reason with certainty. His rupture in 1589 from Kelley, who stayed on in Bohemia to manufacture gold for the Emperor Rudolph the Second while Dee returned to England at the request of Elizabeth, may have inconvenienced his plans. However, it is my contention, as I shall demonstrate in this essay, that Dee was awaiting permission from the angels to employ their magic, and this permission was not given in his lifetime.

THE REALITY OF THE ENOCHIAN ANGELS
It is necessary to state here unequivocally for those unfamiliar with Enochian magic that neither Dee nor Kelley fabricated

the spirit communications. Both believed completely in the reality of the angels, although they differed about the motives of these beings. Dee believed the angels obedient agents of God submissive to the authority of Christ. Kelley mistrusted them and suspected them of deliberate deception. The dislike was mutual. The angels always treated Kelley with amused contempt. Kelley hoped the angels would communicate the secret of the red powder, which is the only reason he endured their insults for so many years.

There is no space here to enter into the entire question of the nature and objective reality of spirits, nor is it likely that any conclusions could be reached on this difficult subject. Whatever their essential nature, the Enochian angels acted as independent, intelligent beings with their own distinct personalities and purposes. This is how Dee and Kelley regarded them, and this is how I shall regard them in this essay, because I am presenting here the secret agenda of the angels, which they concealed from John Dee—to plant among mankind the ritual working that would initiate the period of violent transformation between the present aeon and the next, commonly known in Christianity as the Apocalypse.

The Gates and the Keys

What the Enochian angels conveyed to Dee through Kelley was not merely a more potent form of spirit magic to rule the tutelary daemons of the nations of the earth. It was an initiatory formula designed to open the locked gates of the four great Watchtowers that stand guard against chaos at the extremities of our universe. The Watchtowers are described by the angel Ave:

The 4 houses, are the 4 Angels of the Earth, which are the 4 Overseers, and Watch-towers, that the eternal God in his providence hath placed, against the usurping blasphemy, misuse, and stealth of the wicked and great enemy, the Devil. To the intent that being put out to the Earth, his envious will might be bridled, the determinations of God fulfilled, and his creatures kept and preserved, within the compasse and measure of order.[4]

These Watchtowers, represented in Enochian magic by alphabetical squares, are equivalent to the four mystical pillars of Egyptian mythology that hold up the sky and keep it from crashing into the earth. They bar the chaotic legions of Coronzon from sweeping across the face of the world. Coronzon, the Enochian angels reveal to Dee, is the true heavenly name for Satan.[5] He is also known by the Enochian title of Death-Dragon or Him-That-Is-Fallen (in the Enochian language, Telocvovim).[6]

There is an obvious correspondence between the four Watchtowers and the four archangels of modern Western ceremonial magic, Michael (South), Gabriel (West), Uriel (North), and Raphael (East), who serve as gatekeepers for the four quarters of the earth. Ave's words suggest that these archangels should be regarded not merely as gatekeepers of the quarters, but as the gates themselves.

The Enochian Calls, or Keys (the angels refer to them by both titles), are 48 spirit evocations delivered to Dee and Kelley in the Enochian language and then translated into English word for word by the angels. The overt purpose of the Keys, declared by the angels, is to enable Dee to establish ritual communication with the spirits of the thirty Aethers or Airs who rule over the tutelary daemons of the nations of the earth.

There are actually 49 Keys, but the first, the angels inform Dee, is too sacred and mysterious to be voiced. The first eighteen explicit Keys are completely different from one another in their wording; the last thirty are similar save for the name of the Aether inserted in the first line. It may be that the first eighteen of these invocations should receive the designation Keys, and that the last thirty should more properly be termed Calls. This distinction is usually not made, but it seems to me to make sense.

The angel Raphael declares the expressed purpose of the Keys to Dee:

> In 49 voyces, or callings: which are the Natural Keyes, to open those, not 49. but 48. (for One is not to be opened) Gates of understanding, whereby you shall have knowledge to move every Gate, and to call out as many as you please, or shall be thought necessary, which can very well, righteously, and wisely, open unto you the secrets of their Cities, & make you understand perfectly the [...] contained in the Tables.[7]

The tables referred to by Raphael are the 49 alphabetical tables from which the Keys were generated, one letter at a time, by the Enochian angels. The Keys are probably related in sets to the four Watchtowers, which contain the names of various hierarchies of spirits. A word or words is omitted from Raphael's declaration in Casaubon's book, which I have marked with brackets and an ellipsis. I call this the expressed purpose of the Keys because they have a hidden purpose the angels never state.

Dee's blindness to the true function of the Keys is curious, because clues about their nature are everywhere for those with eyes to see them. The Enochian communications recorded by Dee are filled with apocalyptic pronouncements and imagery. Again and again the angels warn of the coming destruction of the world by the wrath of God and the advent of the Antichrist. This apocalyptic imagery is also found throughout the Keys themselves.

The very name of these evocations should have been clue enough. If the Watchtowers stand guard at the four corners of our dimension of reality, keeping back the hordes of Coronzon from descending like "stooping dragons," as the Eighth Key puts it, and if the evocations known as the Keys are designed to open the gates of these Watchtowers, we might be led to suspect that it would be a bad idea to unlock the gates without applying filters or restrictions on those that pass through.

Perhaps Dee believed, as the angels deceitfully encouraged him to believe, that the gates could be opened a crack for specific human purposes and then slammed shut before anything too horrible slipped through to our dimension of awareness. He would have assumed that the harrowing of the goddess Earth and her children by the demons of Coronzon would not occur until the preordained time of the Apocalypse, an event initiated by God and presumably beyond Dee's control.

What he may have failed to understand is that the date of the initiation of the period of change known as the Apocalypse is (in the intention of the angels) the same date as the successful completion of the full ritual working of the eighteen distinct manifest Keys and the Call of the Thirty Aethers upon the Great Table of the Watchtowers, and that this date is not predetermined, but will be determined by the free will and actions of a single human being who is in the Revelation of Saint John called the Antichrist.

THE NATURE OF THE APOCALYPSE

It has always been generally assumed that the Apocalypse is in the hands of the angels of wrath, to be visited upon the world at the pleasure of God, at a moment foredestined from the beginning of creation. In the veiled teachings of the Enochian angels, this is not true. The gates of the Watchtowers can only be unlocked from the inside. The angels of wrath cannot initiate the Apocalypse even if they wish today to do so. This is suggested by an exchange between Dee and the angel Ave:

Dee—As for the form of our Petition or Invitation of the good Angels, what sort should it be of?

Ave—A short and brief speech.

Dee—We beseech you to give us an example: we would have a confidence, it should be of more effect.

Ave—I may not do so.

Kelley—And why?

Ave—Invocation proceedeth of the good will of man, and of the heat and fervency of the spirit: And therefore is prayer of such effect with God.

Dee—We beseech you, shall we use one form to all?

Ave—Every one, after a divers form.

Dee—If the minde do dictate or prompt a divers form, you mean.

Ave—I know not: for I dwell not in the soul of man.[8]

Spiritual beings who are outside the Watchtowers must be evoked into our reality by human beings. We must open the gates and admit the servants of Coronzon ourselves. Evocation and invocation are not a part of the business of angels, but of humans. That is why it was necessary for the Enochian angels to go through the elaborate ruse of conveying the system of Enochian magic, with the Keys and the Great Table of the Watchtowers, to Dee. If the Apocalypse is to take place, and if it is necessary for human beings to open the gates of the Watchtowers before it can take place, the angels first had to instruct a man in the correct method for opening the gates.

It is evident that Dee was to be restrained from opening the gates of the Watchtowers until it pleased the angels. The angel Gabriel, who purports to be speaking with the authority of God, tells him:

I have chosen you, to enter into my barns: And have commanded you to open the Corn, that the scattered may appear, and that which remaineth in the sheaf may stand. And have entered into the first, and so into the seventh. And have delivered unto you a Testimony of my spirit to come.

For my Barn hath been long without Threshers. And I have kept my flayles for a long time hid in unknown places: Which flayle is the Doctrine that I deliver unto you: Which is the Instrument of thrashing, wherewith

you shall beat the sheafs, that the Corn which is scattered, and the rest may be all one.

(But a word in the mean season.)

If I be Master of the Barn, owner of the Corn, and
deliverer of my flayle: If all be mine (And unto you,
there is nothing: for you are hirelings, whose reward
is in heaven).

Then see, that you neither thresh, nor unbinde,
untill I bid you, let it be sufficient unto you: that
you know my house, that you know the labour I will
put you to: That I favour you so much as to entertain you the labourers within my Barn: For within it
thresheth none without my consent.[9]

Surely nothing could be clearer. Throughout the Enochian communications the angels refer to the Apocalypse
euphemistically as "the Harvest." Here, Enochian magic is
specifically described as the "Instrument of thrashing." Yet
Dee did not comprehend the awesome significance of the
burden that had been laid upon his shoulders. Elsewhere in
the record, the angel Mapsama is just as explicit about the
need for Dee to await permission before attempting to use
the Keys:

Mapsama—These Calls are the keyes into the Gates and Cit-
ies of wisdom. Which [Gates] are not able to be opened,
but with visible apparition.

Dee—And how shall that be come unto?

Mapsama—Which is according to the former instructions:
and to be had, by calling of every Table. You called for wisdom, God hath opened unto you, his Judgement: He hath

delivered unto you the keyes, that you may enter; But be humble. Enter not of presumption, but of permission. Go not in rashly; But be brought in willingly: For, many have ascended, but few have entered. By Sunday you shall have all things that are necessary to be taught; then (as occasion serveth) you may practice at all times. But you being called by God, and to a good purpose.

Dee—How shall we understand this Calling by God?

Mapsama—God stoppeth my mouth, I will answer thee no more.[10]

Despite these hints and many others, the angels never actually came out and told Dee that he was to be the instrument whereby the ritual formula that would initiate the Apocalypse would be planted in the midst of humanity, where it would sit like a ticking occult time bomb, waiting for some clever magician, perhaps guided by the angels, to work it. Dee evidently never received the signal to conduct the Apocalypse Working, as I have named it, in his lifetime. It was to be reserved for another century, and another man. That man was Aleister Crowley.

ENTER, THE GREAT BEAST

Even as a child, Crowley became convinced that he was the Great Beast mentioned in the biblical book of Revelation. He studied magic within the Hermetic Order of the Golden Dawn, then went on to construct his own occult system using an amalgamation of the ritual working of Abramelin the Mage, the *Goetia*, and the Tantric sexual techniques of the German Ordo Templi Orientis, among other sources.

He firmly believed that he was the herald for a new age of strife and destruction that would sweep across the world. He called this age the Aeon of Horus, after the Egyptian god of war. In 1904 in Cairo, Egypt, he received in the form of a psychic dictation from his guardian angel, Aiwass, the bible of this apocalyptic period, *Liber AL vel Legis* (*The Book of the Law*). It sets forth some of the conditions that will prevail in the Aeon of Horus. In it is Crowley's famous dictum: "Do what thou wilt shall be the whole of the Law." [11]

It is highly significant that Crowley never considered himself to be the Antichrist. He is not the central character in the drama of the Apocalypse, but the herald who ushers in the age of chaos. In a very real sense he was the gatekeeper of the Apocalypse. The text of the *Book of the Law* clearly states:

This book shall be translated into all tongues: but always with the original in the writing of the Beast; for in the chance shape of the letters and their position to one another: in these are mysteries that no Beast shall divine. Let him not seek to try: but one cometh after him, whence I say not, who shall discover the key of it all. [12]

Crowley studied and practiced Enochian magic more often and more deeply than any other magician of the Golden Dawn; indeed, more deeply than any other human being who has ever lived prior to his century. About the angelic communications of Dee and Kelley, he writes: "Much of their work still defies explanation, though I and Frater Semper Paratus [Thomas Windram], an Adaptus Major of the A[rgentum] A[strum] have spent much time and research upon it and cleared up many obscure points."[13]

The record of his working of the Enochian Aethers in 1909 in the desert of North Africa is preserved in the document titled *The Vision and the Voice*, first published in 1911.[14] He possessed a profound and broad understanding of ritual magic, an understanding not merely theoretical but practical. No other man of the 20th century was better suited to initiate the Apocalypse Working, even as there had been no man better suited than John Dee in the 16th century to receive it from the Enochian angels. It is significant that Crowley believed himself the reincarnation of Edward Kelley.

I doubt that Crowley ever succeeded in correctly completing the entire Enochian Apocalypse Working—that is, the primal occult Key which is nowhere recorded, the eighteen manifest Keys and the Call of the Thirty Aethers in their correct correspondence with the parts of the Great Table of the Watchtowers—but he may have succeeded in partially opening the gates of the Watchtowers. It is significant that he states, concerning the African working with his disciple Victor Neuburg: "As a rule, we did one Aethyr every day."[15] About the method of working the Keys, the angel Ave tells Dee:

Four days… must you onely call upon those names of God [on the Great Table of the Watchtowers], or on the God of Hosts, in those names:

And 14 days after you shall (in this, or in some convenient place) Call the Angels by Petition and by the name of God, unto the which they are obedient.

The 15 day you shall Cloath yourselves, in vestures made of linnen, white: and so have the apparition, use, and practice of the Creatures. For, it is not a labour of years, nor many dayes.[16]

It seems clear to me that the complete Apocalypse Working, which will be conducted by the Antichrist and will throw wide the gates of the Watchtowers (if we are to believe the intimations of the Enochian angels), must be conducted on consecutive days, one Key per day. I would guess that the unexpressed primordial Key of the Great Mother is the missing ingredient that will complete the Working, but this is a matter of practical magic and there is no space to investigate the details of the Apocalypse Working in this brief essay.

Crowley remained firmly convinced until his death in 1947 that the Aeon of Horus had begun in 1904, precisely at the time he received the *Book of the Law*. He may have been right. The chaotic transition between the old Aeon of Osirus (astrologically speaking, the Age of Pisces) into the new Aeon of Horus (Age of Aquarius) is the duration of the Apocalypse, that period when Coronzon shall rule over the cosmos and visit destruction upon mankind. No one knows how many years this phase of transition from one age to the next will cover, but the Apocalypse is a mental transformation that is presently occurring within the collective unconscious of the human race, as the growing chaos of Western society demonstrates.

A MENTAL ARMAGEDDON

It is common among fundamentalist Christians to believe that the end of the world will be a completely physical event and will be sparked by some horrifying material agent—global thermonuclear war, or the impact of a large asteroid, or a deadly plague.

This supposition is natural in view of the concrete imagery in the vision of Saint John the Divine, the purported author of Revelation. It is in keeping with the materialistic world view of modern society. But nobody stops to consider that this destruction is described by angels, or that angels are spiritual creatures, not physical beings.

In my opinion, the Apocalypse prepared by the Enochian angels must be primarily an internal, spiritual event, and only in a secondary way an external physical catastrophe. The gates of the Watchtowers that stand guard at the four corners of our dimension of reality are mental constructions. When they are opened, they will admit the demons of Coronzon not into the physical world, but into our subconscious minds.

Spirits are mental, not material. They dwell in the depths of mind and communicate with us through our dreams, unconscious impulses, and more rarely in waking visions. They affect our feelings and our thoughts beneath the level of our conscious awareness. Sometimes they are able to control our actions, either partially as in the case of irrational and obsessive behavior patterns, or completely as in the case of full possession. Through us, by using us as their physical instruments, and only through us, are they able to influence physical things.

The Enochian communications teach us that not only must humanity itself initiate the cosmic drama of the Apocalypse through the magical formula delivered to John Dee and Edward Kelley more than four centuries ago, but humans must also be the physical actors that bring about the plagues, wars, and famines described with such chilling eloquence in the vision of Saint John. We must let the demons of Coronzon into our minds by means of a specific ritual working. They will not find a welcome place there all at once, but will worm their way into our subconscious and make their homes there slowly over time. In the minds of individuals who resist this invasion, they will find it difficult to gain a foothold, but in the more pliable minds of those who welcome their influence they will establish themselves readily.

Once they have taken up residence, we will be powerless to prevent them turning our thoughts and actions toward chaotic and destructive ends. These Apocalyptic spirits will set person against person and nation against nation, gradually increasing the degree of madness, or chaos, in human society, until at last the full horror of Revelation has been realized upon the stage of the world. The corruption of human thoughts and feelings may require generations to bring to full fruition. Only after the wasting and burning of souls is well advanced will the full horror of the Apocalypse achieve its final fulfillment in the material realm.

Let us suppose for the sake of argument that the signal for the initiation of this psychic invasion occurred in 1904 when Crowley received the *Book of the Law*, as Crowley himself believed. Crowley's Enochian evocations of 1909 then pried the doors of the Watchtowers open a crack— enough to allow a foul wind to blow into the collective subconscious mind of the human race. This would explain the senseless slaughter of the First World War, and the unspeakable horror of the Nazi Holocaust during the Second World War. It would explain the decline of organized religions and why the cults of materialism and atheism have gained supremacy. It would explain the moral and ethical bankruptcy of modern times and the increase in senseless crimes of violence.

We may not have long to wait before the individual known in the vision of Saint John as the Antichrist, the one foretold in Crowley's *Book of the Law* to follow after the Beast, will succeed in completing the Apocalypse Working that was thrust into the world as a flaming sword by the Enochian angels. Then the gates of the Watchtowers will truly gape wide, and the children of Coronzon will sweep into our minds as crowned conquerors. If this chilling mythic scenario ever comes to pass, the wars of the 20th century will seem bucolic to those who survive the slaughter.

IN CONCLUSION

Having set forth this nightmare prospect, it may be necessary for me to stress in closing this essay that it is only speculation on my part, based on the suggestive language used by the angels in Dee's Enochian diaries, and on the beliefs of Aleister Crowley. I am personally convinced that the angels thought that a complete execution of Enochian magic, in what I have termed the Apocalypse Working, would trigger the Apocalypse—but it does not necessarily follow that the angels were correct in their belief. These beings, whatever they may have called themselves, were spirits, and if the practice of magic teaches us anything, it is that spirits often make errors when predicting events in our material world.

Merely because they called themselves angels should not cause us to blindly assume that everything they spoke was the truth. Edward Kelley never made that mistake, and the more credulous John Dee also had his suspicions about the veracity of their words.

Even if we assume that the angels were correct in their belief that they were conveying the trigger for the Apocalypse to mankind, so that we would initiate our own descent into chaos in the transition between astrological ages, it is very doubtful that anyone will ever succeed in performing the complete Enochian Apocalypse Working. The instructions to Dee about how Enochian magic was to be used were never completed—or, at least, were never written down by Dee in his diaries. The information simply does not exist at present.

It is obvious that working parts of Enochian magic does not precipitate the end of the world, because thousands of magicians have been doing just that for more than a century, ever since the Hermetic Order of the Golden Dawn revived interest in Enochian magic by including it in their esoteric system. Enochian magic has proven to be both potent and useful, and many modern practitioners have embraced it as their favored form of magic.

To any Enochian magicians let me say, continue to work your magic. I am not trying to frighten you. There is no imminent danger. Even if Enochian magic is designed to trigger the Apocalypse, as the angels believed, and even if Crowley in his role as the Great Beast did begin to crack open the gates of the Watchtowers, a psychic transmission of the instructions missing from Dee's diaries is required before it can be fulfilled, and its fulfillment will only be realized by the one Aleister Crowley regarded as his magickal child, the Antichrist.

NOTES

1. Dee's espionage activities are the central concern of Richard Deacon's biography *John Dee: Scientist, Geographer, Astrologer and Secret Agent.*

2. Dee's death is usually placed in December of 1608, but a notation in Dee's private diary by a different hand marks Dee's death on March 26, 1609.

3. Casaubon, p. 174.

4. Ibid., p. 170.

5. Ibid., p. 92.

6. Ibid., p. 207.

7. Ibid., p. 77.

8. Ibid., p. 188.

9. Ibid., p. 161.

10. Ibid., pp. 145–46.

11. Crowley, *Book Of the Law*, ms. pp. 10–11.

12. Ibid., ch. 3, para. 47.

13. Crowley, *Confessions*, p. 611.

14. Crowley, *Vision and the Voice.* See also the *Confessions*, ch. 66.

15. Crowley, *Confessions*, p. 618.

16. Casaubon, p. 184.

Bibliography

Agrippa, Henry Cornelius. *The Fourth Book of Occult Philosophy: the Companion to Three Books of Occult Philosophy.* Edited and annotated by Donald Tyson. Woodbury, MN: Llewellyn, 2009.

———. *Three Books of Occult Philosophy.* Edited and annotated by Donald Tyson. St. Paul, MN: Llewellyn, 1993.

Augustine, Saint. *The City of God Against the Pagans.* Seven volumes. Translated by William M. Green. Cambridge, MA: Harvard University Press, 1957–72.

———. *The City of God.* Translated by Marcus Dods. In *Nicene and Post-Nicene Fathers, First Series*, Vol. 2. Buffalo, NY: Christian Literature Publishing Co., 1887.

Bailey, Alice A. *A Treatise on White Magic, or The Way of the Disciple.* New York: Lucis Publishing Company, 1934.

Bathurst, John. *The Worship of the Serpent Traced Throughout the World.* London: J. G. and F. Rivington, 1833.

Beaumont, John. *An Historical, Physiological, and Theological Treatise of Spirits, Apparitions, Witchcrafts, and Other Magical Practices. Containing an Account of the Genii, or Familiar Spirits, both Good and Bad, that are said to attend Men in this Life, &c.* London: Printed for D. Brown at the Black Swan without Temple-Bar; J. Taylor, at the Ship in St. Paul's Church-Yard; R. Smith, at the Angel without Temple-Bar; F. Coggan, in the Inner-Temple Lane; and T. Browne without Temple-Bar, 1705.

Casaubon, Meric, ed. *A True & Faithful Relation of What Passed for Many Yeers Between Dr. John Dee (A Mathematician of Great Fame in Q. Eliz. and King James Their Reignes) and Some Spirits* [1659]. Glasgow: The Antonine Publishing Company Ltd., 1974.

Charles, Robert Henry, ed. *I Enoch.* Contained in volume 2 of *The Apocrypha and Pseudepigraphia of the Old Testament* (pp. 163–281). Oxford: Clarendon Press, 1913.

Christian, Paul. *The History and Practice of Magic.* New York: Citadel Press, 1963.

Christianson, Scott, and Lowell J. Levine. *Bodies of Evidence: Forensic Science and Crime.* Guilford, CT: The Lyons Press, 2006.

Cicero, Chic, and Sandra Tabatha Cicero. *The Essential Golden Dawn: An Introduction to High Magic.* St. Paul, MN: Llewellyn, 2003.

Crowley, Aleister. *Book of the Law.* Quebec: 93 Publishing, no date.

————. *Book of Thoth*. New York: Weiser, 1974.

————. *The Confessions of Aleister Crowley*. Edited by John Symonds and Kenneth Grant. London: Arkana Books, 1989.

————. *Magick in Theory and Practice*. New York: Dover Publications, 1976.

————. *The Vision and the Voice* [1911]. Los Angeles: Thelema Publishing Co., 1952.

Crowley, Aleister, ed. Translated by S. L. MacGregor Mathers [1904]. *The Goetia: The Lesser Key of Solomon the King*. York Beach, ME: Weiser, 1995.

Deacon, Richard. *John Dee: Scientist, Geographer, Astrologer and Secret Agent*. London: Frederick Muller, 1968.

Decker, Ronald, Thierry Depaulis, and Michael Dummett. *A Wicked Pack of Cards*. New York: St. Martin's Press, 1996.

Dehn, Georg, ed. *Buch Abramelin*. Saarbrücken, Germany: Neue Erde Verlag, 1995.

Elworthy, Frederick. *The Evil Eye: The Origins and Practices of Superstition*. New York: Collier Books, 1970.

Frazer, Sir James G. *The Golden Bough: A Study in Magic and Religion*. Abridged edition. New York: The Macmillan Company, 1951.

Godwin, David. *Godwin's Cabalistic Encyclopedia*. St. Paul, MN: Llewellyn, 1989.

Howe, Ellic. *The Magicians of the Golden Dawn: A Documentary History of a Magical Order, 1887–1923*. New York: Samuel Weiser, 1978.

James I, King. *The Demonology of King James I.* Edited by Donald Tyson. Woodbury, MN: Llewellyn, 2011.

Kelley, Edward. *The Alchemical Writings of Edward Kelly.* Edited by A. E. Waite [1893]. New York: Samuel Weiser, 1970.

Kramer, Heinrich, and James Sprenger. *The Malleus Maleficarum.* Translated into English by Montague Summers from the Latin. New York: Dover, 1971.

Layton, Bentley, trans. *The Gnostic Scriptures: Ancient Wisdom for the New Age.* New York: Doubleday, 1995.

Lévi, Éliphas. *Transcendental Magic.* New York: Weiser, 1979.

Mathers, Samuel Liddell MacGregor [1900]. *The Book of the Sacred Magic of Abramelin the Mage.* New York: Dover Publications, 1975.

———. *The Key of Solomon the King* [1888]. York Beach, ME: Samuel Weiser, 1989.

McPherson, J. M. *Primitive Beliefs in the North-East of Scotland.* London: Longmans, Green and Co., 1929.

Murray, Margaret A. *The God of the Witches* [1931]. London, Oxford and New York: Oxford University Press, 1970.

———. *The Witch-Cult in Western Europe* [1921]. London: Oxford University Press, 1967.

Papus. *Tarot of the Bohemians.* New York: US Games, 1978.

Pelton, Robert W., and Karen W. Carden. *Snake Handlers: God Fearers or Fanatics?* Nashville, TN: Thomas Nelson, 1974.

Peterson, Joseph H. *John Dee's Five Books of Mystery.* Boston, MA and York Beach, ME: Weiser Books, 2003.

Pliny. *Natural History.* Ten volumes. Various translators. Cambridge, MA: Harvard University Press, 1938–62.

Ralegh, Sir Walter. *History of the World.* Contained in volume 2 of *The Works of Sir Walter Ralegh, Kt.* Eight volumes. Oxford: University Press, 1829.

Regardie, Israel. *The Art and Meaning of Magic.* Toddington, UK: Helios Books, 1969. Electronic edition, unpaginated.

Robbins, Rossell Hope. *The Encyclopedia of Witchcraft and Demonology.* London: Spring Books, 1959.

Robinson, James M., ed. *The Nag Hammadi Library in English.* San Francisco: Harper and Row, 1981.

Scot, Reginald. *The Discoverie of Witchcraft* [1584]. New York: Dover Publications, 1972.

Skinner, Stephen, and David Rankine. *The Veritable Key of Solomon.* Woodbury, MN: Llewellyn, 2008.

Smith, George. *The Chaldean Account of Genesis.* New York: Charles Scribner's Sons, 1876.

Tyson, Donald. *Necronomicon: The Wanderings of Alhazred.* St. Paul, MN: Llewellyn, 2004.

———. *New Millennium Magic: A Complete System of Self-Realization.* St. Paul, MN: Llewellyn, 1996.

Waite, Arthur Edward. *The Book of Ceremonial Magic.* An expanded edition of Waite's 1898 work, the *Book of Black Magic and of Pacts.* Secaucus, NJ: Citadel Press, 1961.

———. *The Pictorial Key to the Tarot.* New York: Weiser, 1980.

Westcott, W. Wynn. *Sepher Yetzirah*. New York: Weiser, 1980.

White, Nelson, and Anne Nelson. *Lemegeton: Clavicula Salomonis, or The Complete Lesser Key of Solomon the King*. Photocopy of British Library Sloane 2731, along with a transcription. Pasadena, CA: The Technology Group, 1979.

Index

symbolism, 5, 10, 38, 55–58, 68, 70, 97, 101, 137, 138, 141, 157, 166, 167, 170, 171, 173, 179, 180, 182, 183, 199, 229, 232, 233, 239, 240

synesthesia, 148

T

Tales of Mother Goose (Perrault), 194

Tantra, 8, 267

Tao, 8

Tarot, 12, 17, 18, 37, 133, 155–161, 163, 165–170, 173–179, 181, 184, 188

Tarot of the Bohemians (Papus), 166

tattwa, 38

Tetragrammaton, 58, 229

Thelema, 3, 105

Theosophy, 190

Theurgia Goetia, 213

theurgy, 37

Three Books of Occult Philosophy (Agrippa), 26, 28, 210

Tiamat, 94, 95

Tibet, 8, 113, 123

tourbillion, 66

Tree of Life, 157, 184

triangle, 59, 63, 140, 141, 150, 224, 229–231

trumps, 12, 17, 18, 155–184

tulpa, 123

Tzaddi, 164, 165, 170, 172, 175–178, 185

To Write to the Author

If you wish to contact the author or would like more information about this book, please write to the author in care of Llewellyn Worldwide Ltd. and we will forward your request. Both the author and publisher appreciate hearing from you and learning of your enjoyment of this book and how it has helped you. Llewellyn Worldwide Ltd. cannot guarantee that every letter written to the author can be answered, but all will be forwarded. Please write to:

Donald Tyson
⁒ Llewellyn Worldwide
2143 Wooddale Drive
Woodbury, MN 55125-2989

Please enclose a self-addressed stamped envelope for reply, or $1.00 to cover costs. If outside the USA, enclose an international postal reply coupon.